THE TIMBER PRESS GUIDE TO VEGETABLE GARDENING

in

•SOUTHERN CALIFORNIA•

THE TIMBER PRESS GUIDE TO VEGETABLE GARDENING

in

•SOUTHERN CALIFORNIA•

GERI GALIAN MILLER

Timber Press

Portland, Oregon

Chapter opener illustrations and illustrations on pages 12 and 31 by Julianna Johnson.
Illustration on page 18 by Scott Westgard. Illustration on page 29 by Skye McNeill.
All other illustrations © Julia Sadler

Published in 2015 by Timber Press, Inc.

The Haseltine Building
133 S.W. Second Avenue, Suite 450
Portland, Oregon 97204-3527
timberpress.com

Printed in the United States of America
Book design by Kate Giambrone and Julianna Johnson
Cover design by Bree Goodrow

Library of Congress Cataloging-in-Publication Data

Miller, Geri Galian.

    The Timber Press guide to vegetable gardening in Southern California/Geri Galian Miller.—First edition.
        pages cm
    Other title: Guide to vegetable gardening in Southern California
    Includes index.
    ISBN 978-1-60469-561-8
    1. Vegetable gardening—California, Southern. I. Title. II. Title: Guide to vegetable gardening in Southern California.
    SB321.5.C2M55 2015
    635.09794'9—dc23   2015013387

·TABLE OF·
CONTENTS

Preface

If you're reading this book, you've been blessed to live in the southern part of the Golden State. As diverse a map of topography as it is a map of humanity, Southern California provides vastly different gardening experiences for all 16.5 million of us (that's 43% of the population of the entire state). From the beautiful inland valleys, with their blistering summer heat and potential winter frosts, to the glorious coastal plains, where temperatures rarely reach the extremes of the thermometer, we relish gardening here in USDA zones 9 to 11, and all the a's and b's in between. This book will cover our territory and its various growing regions, starting with the Pacific Coast north of Santa Barbara, at San Luis Obispo, east to just south of Bakersfield, then along the San Gabriel Mountains to San Bernardino and south into San Diego.

Yes, SoCal has it all. Sun and surf, heat and freezes, wind, snow and—well, just a little rain thrown in here and there. Most wonderful of all, though, is that most of us can grow something edible in our gardens 365 glorious days a year! This isn't to say that this near gardening nirvana isn't without its challenges, however. We gardeners still need to develop skills beyond composting. We need to learn how to take our cues from the increasingly unpredictable seasonal shifts that occur here, and be ready to anticipate and deal with the impact of drought and periodic heavy rain on the way we grow food. And what food it is! Our cultural diversity allows us each to share the uniquely personal experience of growing what was familiar to us and our parents and grandparents with our neighbors or fellow community gardeners, and vice versa. It is no surprise then that edible gardens bring people together around food.

Whether you are brand new to gardening or just in need of a refresher, the format of this book makes it easy for you to learn about our unique SoCal growing region, and how climate zones, topography, and changing weather patterns affect our gardening experiences. Included are a primer on the basic tenets of organic gardening, with tips and tricks about planning and planting; a month-to-month guide that delivers practical advice about what you can expect—and do— each month; and, the heart of the matter, Edibles A to Z. A seasoned gardener's mantra is "know what you grow." The Edibles A to Z section gives you everything you'll need to know to successfully grow your tried-and-true favorites and a few new ones that will surprise you! Agretti, dragonfruit, or fenugreek, anyone?

Food security, economic pressures, self-sufficiency, healthier eating, tastier eating, reducing your carbon footprint, family togetherness, community spirit, exercise, stress relief, a landscape that is both beautiful and productive—whatever your reason for choosing to begin your edible gardening adventure, you've joined an incredible group of like-minded folks! Natural nurturers, we edible gardeners support each other's desire to grow what we eat and understand each trial and victory along the way.

But first, a few words on "success" and "failure." Above all, remove any preconceived notions you have of both words, especially when you're a beginner. You know, sometimes we just can't seem to get out of our own way. If you have expectations that your first season gardening or your first season in a new site is going to end in some kind of "coffee table book" garden of Eden, you will be setting yourself up for disappointment. Not

only is gardening on-the-job training, but gardening forces us instant-gratification-loving humans to *slow down* and learn on Mother Nature's timetable, not our own. We learn by reading and discussing with other gardeners, of course, but nothing is a substitute for being out there, observing closely, and getting dirty in your own garden—season after season.

As for "failures," when we were children we really had no fear. As we grew, we developed a fear of peer disapproval if we didn't get things right the first time and soon we began to be afraid of trying new things. How sad is that? I have to quote my dear ol' dad, who taught me that if you don't fail, you don't learn. So, set your fears aside, follow your bliss, and take that first step . . . or shovelful. We're all learning together. And whatever your reason for getting your hands "dirty," this book will become your indispensable, dirt-stained, dog-eared guide and inspiration to get growing all year long!

GET STARTED

WELCOME TO
NIRVANA

Yes, we are golden, with virtually endless growing seasons. But we live in a land of contrasts and, increasingly, surprises. This short chapter will give you some idea of the "typical" climate rhythms of the coastal plains and inland valleys that make up the majority of southern California (then we'll spend the rest of the book looking into how best to cope when they are anything but typical). Using your area's first and last frost dates and the average high and low temperatures as represented by the USDA Plant Hardiness Zone Map (see Resources for the link) may be helpful as a baseline. But more and more, these should be taken, at best, as a very general guideline rather than a solid predictor of temperature highs and lows for your area (down to the zip code), given the changes in climate we've experienced firsthand over the last decade. All seasoned gardeners have been witness to this change and will attest to the necessity of developing skills to evaluate and assess conditions as they happen.

Growing Regions

Literally, you are only an hour or two away from a distinctly different weather experience in SoCal! All the growing regions covered in this book are surrounded by mountain ranges that contribute to our very divergent

San Luis Obispo

Bakersfield

Santa Barbara

Oxnard

Pasadena

Los Angeles

Long Beach

Pacific Ocean

Oceanside

San Diego

weather patterns. These mountain ranges, the Transverse Ranges, are unique in that they run east-west, as opposed to the rest of California's north-south running mountains.

South Coast: San Luis Obispo County and South to San Diego

The coastal regions enjoy a typically mild temperature range. There's not a huge shift between day and night-time temperatures, which allows coastal gardeners to "stretch" the seasons a bit more. Mild temperatures aside, this region is subjected to periods or seasons of fog and high dew point, which can cause a host of fungal diseases if gardeners are not vigilant. Proper irrigation methods and timing are critical to help avoid the spread of these diseases.

One thing has remained nearly constant. Each year, the South Coast endures "June Gloom"—about a month of almost entire days of a thick layer of low clouds. June Gloom forms each year in differing strengths, it begins in late May and can literally hang around, through June

for a certainty but sometimes into July and even August. This weather pattern is caused by the marine layer (a low-hanging "sheet" of stratus clouds) and is amplified by the Catalina eddy (aka coastal eddy). The Catalina eddy is a weather event that occurs when upper level airflow mixes with the Southern California topography of the coastline and islands. When the offshore winds coming from the north and the southern coastal winds hit the mountains of SoCal, they spin the marine layer in a counterclockwise direction, moving the clouds farther inland. In lighter June Gloom years, the marine layer usually stays near the coast, burns off to reveal the bright SoCal sunshine we all love by the early afternoon, and disappears by the end of June. However, in a heavy June Gloom year the clouds can extend into the inland valleys and stick around most of the day. *That* is a summer bummer!

On the up side, the South Coast's growing season is literally 365 days long, with frost events virtually nonexistent or extremely rare. Soil profile in this region is a range of sandy soil along the coastline to heavier clay more inland and on the hills. This area is affected by the Santa Ana wind events several times a year. According to NOAA (again, see Resources for the link) coastal average temperatures range from lows of 43 to 48°F to highs of 71 to 75°F.

Inland Valleys: Santa Clarita, San Fernando, San Gabriel, and Similar Valleys

Southern California valleys are a study in climatic extremes, courtesy of two significant weather influences: cool ocean breezes and hot, drying winds through inland areas. These factors combine with the

DRIVING FORCES

Santa Ana wind events in Southern California can happen multiple times a year from October through March. These winds blow westward from the northeast through inland canyons, carrying hot, dry air toward the coast. Higher temperatures occur with these events, so gardeners, stand ready to guard your plants! They can be desiccated by these winds.

mountainous topography to create multiple micro-climates and a dose of winter chill more significant than that experienced in the coastal areas. On the up side, the seasonal low clouds and fog that plague the coast are less of a factor here.

Frost dangers can range from mild to severe, with hard frosts common in many valleys from November through January. This seasonal variance means you can grow a diverse variety of edibles, from heat-loving summer varieties to fruits demanding a high number of chill hours during the dormant winter months. Another positive! Average temperatures can range from lows of 25 to 35°F to highs of 88 to 100°F and more.

HANDLING THE JUNE GLOOM

In SoCal we can plan on June Gloom every year starting around Memorial Day. When it will end is another thing altogether. Meteorologists tell us that years with warmer ocean temperatures (El Niño) may mean fewer gloomy days in May and June. Cooler ocean temperatures (La Niña) usually mean a more gray beginning to the SoCal summer. In an El Niño year, the June Gloom is less likely to be very heavy in the inland valleys, whereas La Niña can mean significantly grayer days for a longer period of time. Unfortunately, whether it's an El Niño or La Niña, the South Coast will most definitely be gray at this time every year, so be prepared to deal with the effects of this shift, which can jolt you and your plants from a warming spring into a cooler, darker beginning of summer.

GARDENING
101

"What's the secret to a great edible garden?" Gardeners ask this question again and again. As in all things that are important, the answer is both simple and complex. The simple answer is that it's all about the soil, first and foremost. The more complex answer has to do with what great soil really is. Great soil has just a few critical elements: a strong, healthy soil food web, good soil tilth, texture and structure, and an abundance of organic matter.

Soil

Now that you know what makes great soil great, let's get into how to get yours to be great. First things first—you've got to get to know your soil. Learn its strengths and weaknesses, and then set out to make it better, before you plant. Stand in your garden and take a look around; evaluate your landscape. Then you can start digging. Look to see if your soil has these qualities (the more it differs, the more work you have in store):

- Sufficient soil moisture. Enough water is available on a regular basis to support what you want to grow.
- Good water infiltration. Soil should be able to absorb about ½ inch of water per hour in the top 20 inches.
- Adequate drainage. Water drains well through soil; area does not flood, nor does water puddle for extended periods of time.
- Balanced chemistry. The soil pH shouldn't be extremely acidic or alkaline.
- Proper soil depth. There's enough topsoil over bed rock, gravel, or hardpan to allow for root growth and moisture storage.
- Even topography. The more level the garden, the easier the access. Any slopes in your landscape should be gentle, so that the soil doesn't erode easily, creating a runoff problem.
- Lack of rocks. Minimal amount of gravel, stones, or boulders.
- Moderate temperature. Average annual soil temperature should be higher than 32°F and the average summer soil temperature should be higher than 46°F.

A strong, healthy soil food web

The soil food web is the community of organisms that live all or some of their lives in the top 4 to 6 inches of soil. Each organism in this web has a role to play in converting energy and nutrients as one organism eats another; therefore, the health of each organism, from the single-celled to the larger creatures, is vital to soil fertility. Soil organisms support plant health—they decompose organic matter, cycle nutrients, enhance soil structure, and keep the populations of all their fellows, good and bad, in balance. The best way to protect and nurture your soil food web is to add organic compost regularly and avoid using pesticides (even organic ones); do not use synthetic fertilizers, and do not overwork (till) the soil.

Good soil tilth, texture, and structure

The term "tilth" refers to the ability of the soil to support plant and root growth. Soil with good tilth is easy to work, has the ability to successfully germinate seedlings, and allows for good root penetration.

TAKE AN EARTHWORM CENSUS

Choose a 1-foot-square site that is a good average of your garden. Dig out the top 6 inches and place in a shallow pan. Then simply count the number of earthworms in the removed soil by moving the earth around bit by bit.

One or two earthworms, your soil needs some improvement.

Five to nine earthworms, you're getting there, but still need more organic matter.

If you find 10 or more earthworms—congratulations! You have healthy, biologically active soil!

SOIL TEXTURE FIELD TEST

These three simple tests can help you determine your soil's texture while you're in your own backyard. I usually use the ribbon test. A soil test lab can give you a more accurate assessment, but these tests are fully capable of giving you a very good idea of what you are dealing with.

Feel test. Thoroughly dry and crush a small amount of soil by rubbing it with your forefinger in the palm of your other hand. Then rub some of it between your thumb and fingers to measure the percentage of sand. The grainier it feels, the higher the sand content.

Moist cast test. Compress moist soil by squeezing it in your hand. When you open your hand, if the soil holds together (that is, forms a cast), pass it from hand to hand—the more durable the cast, the higher the percentage of clay.

Ribbon test. Roll a handful of moist soil into a cigarette shape and squeeze it between your thumb and forefinger to form the longest and thinnest ribbon possible. Soil with high silt content will form flakes or peel instead of forming a ribbon. The longer and thinner the ribbon, the higher the percentage of clay.

   For the moist cast and ribbon tests, the soil specimen should be gradually moistened and thoroughly reshaped and kneaded to bring it to its maximum "plasticity" and to remove dry lumps. Do not add too much water, as the sample will lose its cohesion.

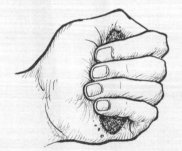
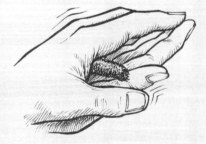

Moist cast (left) and ribbon tests

Soil texture refers to the size of the particles that make up your soil. Soil texture has a major effect on the physical properties of soil. As soil particles get larger, the spaces between the particles get bigger. Clay has the smallest particles, silt's particles are medium-sized, and sand has the largest particles, which is the major reason water drains through it so easily (greatest pore space) and why clay drains so slowly (smallest pore space). Soil texture dictates not only how well your soil drains but also how well it retains nutrients and moisture. Clay soils tend to be fertile but drain poorly. Sandy soils drain easily but tend to dry out quickly and be less fertile. Loams retain moisture and are fertile and friable (crumbly and easy to work). Many plants tolerate a variety of soil textures, while some, like edibles, have more specific soil requirements. The vast majority of edibles do best in lighter loamy soils, which are about 40% sand, 40% silt, and 20% clay.

Structure refers to how the soil particles hang together in clods or crumbs—or not. Good soil structure can compensate for less-than-perfect soil texture. Whatever your soil texture, loose crumbs and clods ensure good pore spaces. Routinely adding an abundant amount of organic matter is the surest way of attaining (and keeping) good soil structure as well as overall soil health and fertility. For edibles, the recommended amount of compost to add the first season is 3 to 4 inches. You can decrease the amount of compost you add in subsequent seasons, as your soil improves, to a 2-inch layer as a mulch applied once a season.

Understanding soil pH

An important factor in the availability of soil nutrients to plants is the degree of acidity or alkalinity of the soil, as measured by pH (potential hydrogen). The pH scale ranges from 0 to 14, with 7.0 being neutral, lower numbers being acidic, and higher numbers being alkaline. At pH extremes, some nutrients become partially or completely locked up in the soil and cannot be used by plants, even though they are all present in adequate amounts. Most edibles thrive in a soil pH of 6.5 to 7.5 (slightly acid to neutral).

Siting Your Garden

Location, location, location: as in real estate, so it is in the garden! Choosing the best location for your garden will mean the difference between success and failure. Now that you have considered your soil, it's time to make sure the microclimate and exposure of your proposed garden site is right for edibles.

Microclimate

A microclimate is the climate of a small area that is different from the areas around it. It may be warmer or colder, wetter or drier, windy or still, or more or less prone to frosts. Try to identify the microclimates on the proposed site (yes, there can be more than one). Are buildings, structures, or trees creating microclimates that are hotter, colder, more moist than the rest of the site? A protected courtyard next to a building, for example, is warmer than an exposed field nearby. By going out to your proposed site at different times of the day and evening and documenting your observations, you'll be able to develop a record of the effects of the microclimate in that area.

Exposure

You've probably all heard that edibles need full sun to be successful. You're probably asking yourself (never minding that you might not know exactly what full sun meant), "But what if I have only part sun or part shade? Can I still have edibles in my garden?" The answer, anxious gardeners, is a resounding yes! Understanding your exposure is the key.

Full sun. The generally accepted definition of full sun is 6 or more hours of direct sunlight per day. But here's where gardeners need to understand the one factor that is rarely mentioned: the time of day that the light is hitting the plant. There are 4 key hours in the full sun equation, 11 a.m. to 3 p.m. (give or take a half-hour on either side). That's when the sun is most powerful. Having said that, the intensity of your full sun in, say, a coastal community is not the same thing as full sun in an inland valley location. These climates zones are different. Also, don't forget the seasonal position of the sun—high in the sky in summer, lower in the sky in winter.

WIND: ANOTHER "ASPECT" TO KEEP IN MIND

Edibles can be very vulnerable to drying winds. Is the proposed site subjected to wind events (sporadic or constant)? Are natural wind buffers present (hedges, trees)? If you are considering a windy site, you'll have to provide some kind of windbreak, either trees or shrubs or a physical barrier (fence, wall).

SHADE-TOLERANT EDIBLES

beans	French tarragon
beets	garlic
broccoli	leafy greens (Asian
Brussels sprouts	greens, kale)
cauliflower	parsnips
chard	peas
cilantro	salad greens (arugula,
dill	lettuce, radicchio)
fenugreek	thyme

If you're gardening in the summer in a hot inland valley location, a spot in your yard that receives direct sunlight from 2 p.m. to sunset—just under 6 hours—is not technically full sun, but because the heat index, climate, and humidity levels are different in the late afternoon vs the late morning/early afternoon, plants that would otherwise require full sun would do better sited in an area of your yard that receives part sun. Understanding this is key to siting your plants properly. It may take a few failures to learn this, but don't get discouraged!

Part sun. The classic definition of part sun is a patch of garden that receives either 4 to 5 hours of morning sun, then shade the rest of the day, or shade in the morning, then 4 to 5 hours of sun in the afternoon. If a plant needs part sun, 6 hours or more of direct sunlight that includes high midday sun is too much: the plant will struggle and perhaps its leaves will burn. Anybody remember planting your lettuce in an area like this, only to see its leaves collapse and wilt?

Part shade. Basically it's the same as part (or filtered) sun. Remember, shade is light that is not direct. Even in the various degrees of shade, if the sun is in the sky, its rays are always hitting the plant's leaves, just more weakly. Shade cast by a building is a heavier filter of the sun's rays than all but the thickest tree canopy. So when factoring shade, you must consider both hours of direct sunlight and hours of filtered sun, and learn which plants handle what.

Any further degree of shade is not going to be suitable for edibles.

Water

A happy plant is a well-watered plant, but let's acknowledge that water will not simply fall from the sky, in sufficient amounts, at the right time. Proper irrigation techniques are essential: drip systems, rain catchment systems, and yes, even watering by hand. An edible garden that is kept properly irrigated is a healthy and productive garden. The secret, now that you know your soil texture, climate/microclimate, and exposure, is adjusting the delivery, frequency, and duration of water accordingly.

How soil texture affects watering

We've already learned that particle size differentiates soil textures from each other, giving each different moisture- and nutrient-holding capabilities. Clay, having the smallest particle size, hangs together so tightly, there is very little pore space in between, which gives clay soil its poor drainage and decreased aeration but excellent nutrient-holding characteristics. Silt, having a medium particle size, drains a bit faster than clay and has better nutrient- and water-holding capabilities than sand. Sand, having the largest particle size, drains the fastest but has poor water- and nutrient-holding capabilities. Whether your soil has more or less of one of these three textures determines how fast or slow water will drain through it, which will impact how often and how much you water.

Methods of watering

There are three basic methods of irrigating: hand watering, soaker hoses and drip systems, and movable sprinklers. The method you choose will depend on your lifestyle (do you travel frequently?), available time for garden chores, and budget.

Hand watering. While certainly the most cost-effective, there are costs of a different kind associated with watering this way.

Hand watering is the most cost-effective way to irrigate, but it has its down sides.

- Goof-ups galore. This method is the most prone to human error, as adequate water penetration always takes longer than you think it does. Try this: water your garden with a hose for about 3 minutes, taking care to evenly distribute the water (harder to do than you think). Now stick your finger down into your soil. How far down has the water penetrated? Probably not as deep as you expected. This isn't terrible while your plants are babies with shallow root systems, but it won't be such a good thing when your plants mature and attempt to develop deeper roots.

- Turns you into a watering zombie. Shallow irrigation keeps the moisture near the top of the soil, where it dries out the fastest, and isn't anywhere near your growing plants' potential rooting depth. Over time this encourages the roots to remain shallow, increasing the risk of plant failure, wasting water, and committing you to an unending cycle of more frequent hand watering.

- You need to be around (or the best friend or neighbor you choose to burden when you're not needs to be). Since you're the key to this method it can seriously cramp your travel plans *and* as long as it took you to learn to do it right, how can you expect a newbie to do it right for you?

Soaker hose and drip irrigation. Ok, now we're talking! Though this will mean a bit of cost and initial set up time, you'll find that it will more than make up for this by reduced plant loss and water waste—and a huge saving of your time in the long run.

The configuring of your drip system (type of line and emitters used) will be dictated by your soil texture,

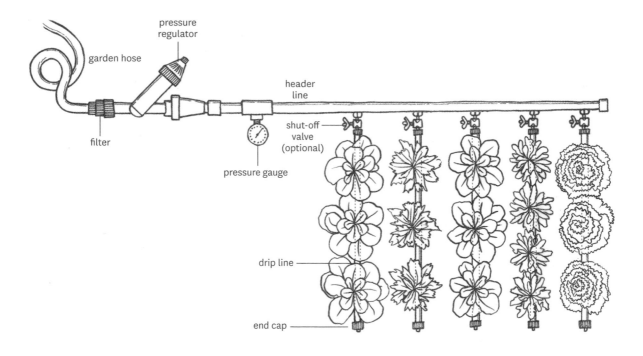

A drip irrigation system

plant palette, and planting scheme. There are literally dozens of different types of lines and emitters available, meaning you can customize your system to address your site's specific needs and you have the flexibility to adapt your system to your plants' changing needs as they grow. Because this approach avoids or keeps wetting foliage to a minimum, drip irrigation helps cut down on the incidence of fungal disease.

Now, here is how this soil texture factors into this. Remember the three textures—sand, silt, and clay? The wetting pattern for each texture is different due to the different sizes of pore space in each. Because sandy soil has the largest pore space, water soaks almost vertically straight down, soaking just a narrow band of soil, hence you'll need to place your emitters or soaker lines closer together. The heavier your soil (the more silt and clay there is), the more distance there can be between your emitters or soaker lines: because there is more capillary action on the horizontal plane, the water will move in a wider swath.

Add a timer to your system and you're free of watering woes—well, almost. Drip systems are wonderful but are not totally maintenance-free. The small holes in drip lines and emitters can get clogged with soil, fertilizers, and minerals, and lines can degrade and be damaged over time. So periodic auditing is going to be needed.

Movable sprinklers. This is the least preferable option as it wastes more water and increases the incidence of disease and pest infestations. Add in wind drift and evaporation, and it is like throwing your money down the drain! In short, whenever budget allows, I recommend a drip system for edibles.

Rain catchment systems

Many of us reap great harvests from our garden. What about harvesting rain? Yes, harvest our rain! Collecting rainwater is not a new concept. Historical records show that rainwater was collected in simple clay containers as far back as 2000 years ago. Maybe it's time to put some of these ancient techniques of rainwater harvesting back into practice!

A few cautionary notes about the safety of rooftop runoff—especially if you're thinking of irrigating edibles. You'll have to evaluate if your roof is a safe source to collect runoff and use straight from a rain barrel for nonpotable uses (I am not talking about these roof systems being used to provide drinking water). Enameled steel and glazed tile roofs generate little or no

Be water-wise! One way to harvest rainwater is to divert a downspout into a rain barrel.

contamination, and rainwater harvested from them is commonly considered safe. Roofs made from the following are *not* candidates for rainwater collection:

- old tar and gravel
- asbestos shingles
- treated cedar shakes
- zinc (galvanized metal) anti-moss strips (usually mounted at the roof peak)
- roofs treated with moss-, lichen-, or algae-killing chemicals within the last several years

Note: Some newer asphalt shingles have zinc particles embedded in the surface. Check your shingle specifications if you have recently re-roofed.

Of course, the location of your home should also be considered. If you live in an industrialized area or near an airport, your roof may collect heavy metal residue from the air. Talk to your local city water agency about any environmental contaminants in your area that may affect rainwater quality. Adding a filtration system to your rain barrel can help reduce these contaminants to below EPA standards.

Opinions differ about whether or not rooftop runoff is safe to use in food gardens. Do your own research, talk to your local water district or county, have your runoff tested (contact your county's public health department), and then decide if you feel comfortable using your rooftop-collected rainwater in your garden. Check with your city or county, as they may have prohibitions on the use of rooftop collected rainwater to irrigate food gardens. Most websites say there hasn't been research done to measure risk effectively, and since much has to do with conditions at the individual location, I doubt there will be. It is because of this that I don't recommend rooftop runoff collection for use in food gardens in schools, especially because the location, maintenance, and age of these facilities are often huge factors.

Cistern systems. A rainwater cistern is a setup for collecting rainwater and storing it until it's needed. A cistern works in a similar way to a rain barrel, only it's bigger and can be above or below ground. Cisterns are a good option when you need to collect and store greater quantities of water.

Graywater systems. Graywater is any non-industrial wastewater generated from household sources such as sinks, washing machines, showers, and bathtubs. Graywater systems allow you to recycle the water that goes down your bathtubs, showers, and laundry for use in your garden. Again, as in the use of rain barrels or cisterns, you need to consider these safety issues:

- Use graywater from bathroom sinks, tubs, showers, and washing machines and avoid graywater from kitchen sinks, dishwashers, and toilets.
- Don't use liquid fabric softener or harsh detergents. Look for biodegradable, low-sodium detergents without phosphates, brighteners, boron, borax, enzymes, or bleach.
- Avoid storing graywater.
- Apply graywater directly to the soil, not by spraying.
- Root crops that are eaten uncooked should not be irrigated with graywater. (California's code states: "Graywater shall not be used to irrigate root crops or edible parts of food crops that touch the soil.")
- Don't use graywater on young plants or plants that like acidic conditions.
- Water from laundry that includes diapers should not be used.
- Don't use graywater when members of the household have a communicable disease such as staph or hepatitis.

Local rules may be even more restrictive than state rules. Check with your local health jurisdiction before planning a graywater reuse system. You should consult with a certified graywater installer or plumber and your local authorities before you install this system. Graywater tends to be alkaline and high in sodium. Acid-loving plants or plants that don't tolerate salinity will not tolerate being irrigated with graywater. You should intermittently irrigate with regular water to flush out the sodium so that it will not build up in the soil.

Fertilizing

Your efforts to build a healthy, vibrant soil food web are about to pay off! When you follow organic soil management strategies, over time you will build soil so naturally fertile, it will require you to intervene much less often with supplemental organic fertilizer—saving time, money, and the environment. It should be every gardener's goal to strive for balance in the garden, adopting the "room for everything" philosophy of organic practice.

With the discovery of synthetic nitrogen in the middle of the last century, we started down a path that would be both a blessing and a curse for the agricultural industry and our environment. Although we were able to feed an ever-growing population (both nationally and globally) with the use of cheaper and faster-acting synthetic nitrogen, we also put in motion environmental impacts that would contribute to the degradation of both our farmland soil and the health of our water systems—a degradation that continues to this day. When large amounts of nitrogen collect in a body of water, an algal bloom is created. The algae rapidly deplete all the oxygen in the water, making it impossible for fish

and other aquatic organisms to survive—which leads to deadly Red Tides and Dead Zones. Our Pacific Ocean is not immune.

Go organic!

The use of inorganic fertilizers alters an ecosystem. Although it seems counterintuitive, synthetic fertilizers decrease soil fertility over time by "breaking" the natural relationship between the nitrogen-fixing microorganisms, plants, and soil, which in turn depletes the store of

Q&A ON NITROGEN

Q: How much nitrogen are we talking about?
A: Nitrogen makes up 78% of the planet's atmosphere.
Q: What is nitrogen used for?
A: Nitrogen is an important part of many organic molecules. It forms a critical part of amino acids and DNA. Nitrogen is essential for all living cells.
Q: What is the nitrogen cycle?
A: It's a 3 step continuous loop:

1 Nitrogen enters the food chain via nitrogen-fixing bacteria and algae in the soil (remember the soil food web?). Once it is "fixed" in the soil by these bacteria, it is in a form that is available for plant's root systems to take up (nitrates). This symbiotic relationship creates and sustains the natural fertility in the soil.

2 The nitrates are processed by the plants to form proteins, which eventually are eaten by decomposers, then grazers, and so on up through the food chain.

3 When these organisms excrete waste, nitrogen is then released back into the atmosphere.

organic matter and microbial populations. Organic fertilizers "build" soil by increasing organic matter and the populations of helpful soil bacteria, both of which help to provide the nutrients plants need to grow naturally.

You have a lot of options when it comes to organic fertilizer. Keep in mind that because their components are found in nature, organic fertilizers take much longer to have an effect than synthetic ones, but this is actually much healthier for your plants. Triggering new growth slowly rather than quickly means that your plant is less likely to attract an infestation of pests or diseases and has more time to develop its critical support systems, such as a vibrant root network and a "ready for anything" immune system. Your choices will be guided by personal preferences, but just know—there is an organic option for everyone!

How much and why?

A few things will determine how much fertilizer to apply to a garden: soil test results; the amount of organic matter present; the natural fertility of the soil; the type of fertilizer you use; and the crop being grown.

If you're unsure of the soil you're about to plant in, doing a soil test is a good idea not only to determine fertility but also to uncover what man-made things, like heavy metals, might be lurking there. Living in Southern California means that much of our land has been used for various industrial or agricultural endeavors at one time or another. If you're at all concerned about your soil's history (industrial contamination), send a sample for heavy metal analysis to your local extension agent or a private lab. Soil test kits for simple fertility/pH analysis can be purchased from garden shops and catalogs.

Healthy, fertile soil will contain both macronutrients (the nutrients plants need the most of) and micronutrients

(aka: trace elements—the nutrients plants need just a little of). Macronutrients are nitrogen, potassium, calcium, magnesium, phosphorus, and sulfur; micronutrients are chlorine, iron, boron, manganese, zinc, copper, molybdenum, and nickel. Of the macronutrients, we are most familiar with the "big" three: nitrogen, phosphorus, and potassium (N-P-K), because they are the ones that are noted in the nutrient content analysis on the front of every box or bag of fertilizer. A general rule of thumb is that nitrogen (the most mobile of the three) is for leafy top growth; phosphorus is for root, bloom, and fruit production; and potassium is for cold hardiness, disease resistance, and general durability. Different edibles require different amounts of nutrients to thrive—another reason "know what you grow" is so crucial!

DIFFERENT EDIBLES, DIFFERENT FEED NEEDS

In general, greens are medium to heavy feeders. Others break down as follows:

Low-demand edibles. Arugula, beans, beets, carrots, fava beans, herbs (most kinds), kale, parsnips, peas, tomatillos, turnips (greens).

Medium-demand edibles. Artichokes, basil, broccoli (sprouting), Brussels sprouts (late), cilantro, corn, cucumber, eggplant, garlic, lettuce, okra, onions, potatoes, tomatoes, turnips (autumn), watermelon.

High-demand edibles. Asparagus, broccoli (raab), Brussels sprouts (early), cauliflower, celery, leeks, peppers, turnips (spring).

When to fertilize? Watch your plants!

Plants send out signals when something is wrong. Learning to read those signals will help you add fertilizers only when your plant tells you it needs it. This will help you keep your garden in balance. Here are the big three deficiencies, and a few signs that point to them.

Nitrogen deficiency. Stunted growth: Plants are not progressing well, are not developing expected size or leaf canopy. Yellowing leaves: Insufficient nitrogen causes a lack of chlorophyll; the leaves will develop a yellowing pattern, noticeable first in the tips and in the margins of older leaves.

Phosphorus deficiency. Stunted growth: Plants have spindly stalks; are not attaining expected size. Odd coloration patterns in leaves: Purple veining may appear on both the top and bottom of the leaves, affecting old and new leaves alike; you may also see bluish green tinting of the older leaves. Decreased blooming/fruiting: Plants have little or no bloom.

Potassium deficiency. Leaf discoloration: Older leaves will be affected first, showing light green to yellow discoloration followed by scorching of the edges and tips. This deficiency can be mistaken for some fungal diseases, so doing a soil test first is advisable; potassium is usually found in adequate amounts in most soils but can be in short supply in sandy soil.

HOW TO SIDE-DRESS FERTILIZER

Side-dressing refers to giving growing plants, especially vegetables, an extra dose of fertilizer, beyond whatever food you may have applied when you planted them. Side-dressing keeps plants growing well and can result in a better harvest.

Side-dress individual plants by applying the fertilizer to the soil and gently scratching it in around each plant at the drip line (as far out as the outermost leaves), being careful not to disturb roots. Water in.

Side-dress rows of plants by scratching the fertilizer into the soil about 6 inches from the row and down the whole length. Water in.

SIDE-DRESS

- fruiting plants when they start to bloom
- broccoli, cabbage, and cauliflower when heads begin to form
- corn when plants are knee-high and silk begins to show
- onions when plants are 6 inches tall, continuing every few weeks until bulb begins to swell

Planting Strategies

Selecting a planting strategy is another important part of being a successful organic gardener. Not only will the right one help you fulfill your garden goals (yield, aesthetics), they can also help you avoid pests and diseases.

Biointensive

This method of raising food (aka French bio-intensive gardening) is based on building and maintaining soil fertility and using no synthetic chemicals. Simple to learn and use, it is based on sophisticated principles dating back 4000 years in China, 2000 years in Greece, and 300 years in Europe. It was synthesized and brought to the United States by English horticulturist Alan Chadwick. Biointensive agriculture has many advantages. It increases yield by 2 to 6 times, reduces energy demands, uses water 3 to 8 times more efficiently, and provides self-contained closed-loop fertility. Its major components are raised beds, intensive or close plant spacing, companion planting, compost, sustainable soil fertility, and open-pollinated seeds (heirlooms, not hybrids).

Companion planting

Companion planting (aka intercropping, bio-diverse planting) is an ancient farming method of planting different species in close proximity to enhance and

An example of companion planting: young broccoli plants and mature tomatoes

support each other. The classic New World example of companion planting is the Three Sisters (planting corn, pole beans, and squash together): the corn provides support for the pole beans; the pole beans enrich the soil by fixing nitrogen from the air into the root zone, so that it is easily taken up by the corn's roots; and the squash's big leaves shade the feet of the corn and beans to slow the evaporation of moisture from the soil. Here in SoCal, I scatter-plant onions and their relatives among other plants, especially in the lettuce patch, as alliums can deter pests like aphids and Japanese beetles. When you choose companion planting (what every vegetable patch is, really—monocultures of homegrown edibles are rare), you also create habitats for beneficial insects or animals, keep the number of problem pests in check, promote biodiversity, and enrich your soil to create a living ecosystem of beneficial bacteria and helpful fungi. For me, and the clients I garden with, this is the only way to garden: in concert with Mother Nature.

Crop rotation

Here's a key strategy: don't grow plants in the same place where they or a member of their family grew last year! Using a sound crop rotation schedule will help you avoid diseases that can plague certain plants—like the dread late blight on your tomatoes or potatoes (the pathogen in this case can live on undecomposed plant tissues left behind in the soil). Another benefit is that soil tilth is improved by rotating plants of various rooting depths (see sidebar in July for more on these). The ideal rotation schedule is a 3-year plan, because even that can get complicated in a smaller area with a diverse planting scheme. Here is a simple rotating plan for tomatoes, beans, and zucchini.

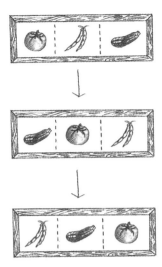

Pests and Diseases

There is no guarantee that once you establish an organic system, you will never face a disease or insect problem. Stressful conditions that you cannot control will happen—droughts, extreme temperatures, insect infestations, fungal diseases floating in on the air. However, with careful observation, preparation, and adherence to a solid organic practice, your garden should experience decreasing pest and disease issues as the years go by.

In the meanwhile, who's eating your garden? If not you, then who? Yes, pests will happen, and they should! As organic gardeners, we strive for balance in our gardens, and that means the goal is controlling (not eliminating) the populations of what we call "pests." Insects (even the ones we call pests) are important in our gardens. Yes, they eat the plants we love, but they also prey on other insects, help pollinate our flowers, decompose plant matter, and even help spread seeds. If we work to eliminate these "pests," our gardens are no longer in balance, as the beneficial insects that we do want in our gardens no longer have anything to prey upon. No, instead we make room for all in our gardens—pollinators, beneficials, and, yes, pests.

And you're in luck! If you've been working hard, following good organic practice, you're already on your way to a healthy garden, and a healthy garden is less likely to be troubled by pests. If it is, use only organic pesticides, and even those sparingly (and again: *never* when pollinators or beneficials are active).

The first step in pest control is identifying what type of pest is doing the damage. The culprit might not always be obvious. That's when being familiar with the particular type of damage different "bad" pests make can be the key to garden success.

WHAT TO DO ABOUT PROBLEM PESTS

Most insect damage is caused by soft-bodied pests (aphids, spider mites, caterpillars) or snails and slugs. Pests can usually be controlled effectively by first adjusting anything that we are doing that may contribute to the problem (overwatering, overfertilizing, spacing the plants incorrectly, watering late in the day) and then? Besides handpicking, you can always . . .

- Use an organic insecticidal soap on aphids and other soft-bodied insects.
- Use an organic insecticidal spray with pyrethrins on beetles or other hard-bodied insects.
- Use an organic pelleted nontoxic desiccant for snails and slugs.

Pests that literally "suck" are many, including aphids, spider mites, stink bugs, thrips, and whiteflies. Some signs of sucking damage: stem and leaf distortion, including leaf spotting, stippling, curling, or puckering; off-color leaves; galls (swellings on leaves and stems); and damaged (or even split) stems. Sucking insects can carry and transmit disease, so controlling them is critical.

Regularly observe for caterpillars, beetles and their grubs, and other chewing pests. They damage roots and stems and eat holes in flowers and leaves. **TIP** More symmetrical holes in flowers and middle of leaves are likely to be caterpillars—watch for their frass (excrement).

Cabbageworm larvae chew large, irregular holes, usually in the middle of leaves, and bore into mature heads, where they drop greenish brown fecal pellets. Seedlings too may be damaged.

Cutworms attack most garden crops. They clip off seedling stems near or just below the soil level, and sometimes chew holes in leaves, young fruit, or vegetables. Fruiting stems wilt and fall.

Flea beetles get their name from their prominent hind legs, and when they are disturbed they jump like fleas. They are common pests of seedling tomatoes. Adult beetles chew small pinholes in the leaves, giving them a sieve-like appearance.

Snails and slugs feed on a variety of living plants and on decaying plant matter. They chew irregular holes with smooth edges on the outer margin of leaves and flowers and can clip succulent plant parts. They can also chew fruit. Their silvery trails are hard to miss!

BENEFICIALS WE LOVE, OR LADY BUG, LADY BUG, DON'T FLY AWAY HOME

What would a garden be without buzzing bees, fluttering butterflies, delicate spider webs, the rainbow dart of a dragonfly? Not very productive for sure! Did you know that of all the insects known to us, less than 1% are categorized as pests? That leaves a lot of "good guys" out there. Here are some of the most common.

- **Assassin bugs** feed on a wide array of small- to medium-sized insects, including caterpillars and aphids (but also lacewings and other beneficials, alas).
- **Damsel bugs** feed on thrips, spider mites, aphids, and small caterpillars.
- **Ground beetles**. Often found under mulch, these large shiny beetles eat slugs, snails, and caterpillars.
- **Hoverflies** resemble bees; they eat aphids and other small insects.
- **Lacewings** are brown or green with transparent wings; they enjoy devouring aphids, thrips, spider mites, and insect eggs.
- **Lady beetles**, aka lady bug. This beloved beneficial goes after aphids, thrips, whiteflies, spider mites, and other soft-bodied insects.
- **Parasitic wasps** are among the most effective natural enemies of aphids: they lay their eggs inside aphids.
- **Praying mantis**. Mantids feed on many different kinds of insects, including other beneficials and even other mantids!
- **Spiders**. General all-around good garden friends. Let them be!
- **Tachinid flies**. Look like hairy houseflies; eat caterpillars, cabbageworms, cutworms.

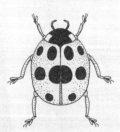

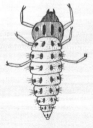

Life cycle of the lady beetle, aka lady bug

Composting

The best compost is the compost you make yourself. Not only do you control exactly what is in it, but you also have the joy of knowing that you're taking another step toward reducing your carbon footprint, through recycling. Composting is a natural recycling process, the decomposition of organic material—leaves, plant tissue, insects/animals, even kitchen scraps. What is left is a rich soil amendment that gardeners fondly nickname "Black Gold," a reference to the way humus looks (fine, black crumbles). Humus is the technical name for compost in its final stage of decomposition. Bacteria, fungi, and worms, among others, are what break down dead plants, animals, and insects. This cast of composting characters is called decomposers. Decomposition happens when these organisms are exposed to a balance of oxygen, moisture, and nutrients. There are three types of composting:

- Aerobic (= in the presence of oxygen). This is how most people compost: it's faster and more efficient than other methods, and it smells better (if done correctly). Generates heat of 140 to 160°F or higher, which is hot enough to kill most pathogens and seed. The pile must be turned regularly to introduce more oxygen and keep the temperature in the core of the pile high.

TYPES OF COMPOSTING SYSTEMS

Single bin. The most common and inexpensive system, usually made of plastic or wood. You can build your own, or check with your city: many have discounted bins available to promote home composting.

Multi-bin. This is a large system usually using three compartments. Compartments are filled as ingredients become available. Usually by the time the second compartment is full, the first compartment's batch is done.

Tumbler. This tends to be an expensive system (although you can make one yourself), on a smaller scale. What it lacks in size, it makes up for in efficiency. We use a tumbler system in our urban farm that has dual insulated chambers. We get completed compost in about 4 weeks!

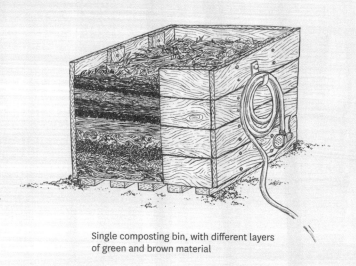

Single composting bin, with different layers of green and brown material

- Anaerobic (= in the absence of oxygen). Aka passive composting. Slow and can stink. The rotten-egg smell is caused by hydrogen sulfide.
- Vermicomposting. Aka cold composting. In this type of composting, red wiggler worms and accompanying mircoorganisms process organic matter. The worms are space-efficient (perfect for apartment dwellers), fast (1000 worms can eat roughly one pound of organic waste each week), and odor-free.

How to do it

As in all gardening, balance is the secret to success when it comes to your (let's assume aerobic) compost pile. For the natural decomposition process to work well, we must create a balanced environment in which the living organisms (the decomposers) will thrive. This means that the pile requires four equally important things to work effectively:

- Carbon for energy. The microbial oxidation of carbon produces the heat, if included at correct levels. High-carbon materials tend to be brown and dry.
- Nitrogen to grow and reproduce more organisms to oxidize the carbon. High-nitrogen materials tend to be green (or colorful, such as fruits and vegetables) and wet.
- Oxygen for oxidizing the carbon, the decomposition process.
- Water in the right amounts to maintain activity without causing anaerobic conditions.

The pile must be kept evenly moist (like a wrung-out sponge) and well oxygenated (turned frequently), and the carbon/nitrogen ratio must be in the right proportions. While the first two are pretty simple, the

---

COMPOST MATERIALS: DO ADD . . .

GREEN	BROWN
food scraps*	dry leaves
all veggies	aged hay
fruit wastes (keep citrus to a minimum)	cardboard egg containers
coffee/tea grounds	newspaper (soy ink)
spent flowers	wood chips/twigs (small pieces)
alfalfa meal or hay	straw
bone meal	paper towels (not bleached)
feathers/hair	shredded paper
fresh grass	dried grass
chicken manure	wood ash (not too much)
humus	coffee filters (not bleached)
weeds	sawdust
rotted manure	tea bags

* Old bread and eggshells are good, but eggshells (like corncobs) take a long time to break down. You get faster results if everything you add is chopped up into finer pieces or shreds. The smaller going in, the faster coming out!

COMPOST MATERIALS: DON'T ADD . . .

- meat
- fish
- bones
- fatty or oily foods
- dairy products
- pesticide-ridden foods
- pet manure

How not to stink at it, you ask? Easy! Here are the compost no-nos:

- Don't keep your pile too wet (remember, wrung-out sponge!).
- Don't let your C/N ratio get out of balance (too much green and you'll stink!).
- Don't neglect to turn your pile (no oxygen in your pile means things will slow down, and you'll stink!).
- Don't add any plant materials that are diseased.
- Don't add woody materials in big pieces: they don't break down very fast.

When is it done?

Your compost is done when it looks, feels, and smells like healthy earth. The consistency should be crumbly and the color dark. Its particles should be able to pass through a ⅜-inch screen (what we use to sift out the remaining big chunks of materials). This is humus—the final result of decomposition. Quality compost should have a pH 6.8 to 7.3.

balance between carbon and nitrogen ingredients is what trips up most would-be home composters. Eyes glazed over yet? No worries. This isn't a perfect world so your compost won't be either, but if you try to keep to a 2:1 ratio—2 parts green (nitrogen) to 1 part brown (carbon)—you should be fine. In my experience, even a 1:1 ratio works, just not as fast.

GARDEN
PLANNING

Gardeners can sometimes get carried away when planting gardens. We're just crazy that way! Like hitting the aisles of a grocery store when you're hungry, shopping for the next season's edibles can easily sweep you off your feet. Before you realize it, you've overspent and, sometimes, overplanted. With a little restraint and a dash of a reality check, you can avoid overwhelming yourself, your pocketbook, and your garden.

Deciding What to Grow

You've heard for years from chefs and food reformers that eating locally and seasonally is the best way to eat, both from a nutrition/flavor standpoint but also from the aspect of sustainability and our carbon footprint. When you grow your own food, you learn quickly about seasonality and the "what grows when" of edibles. Generally, edibles fall into two categories: cool- and warm-season.

Warm-season crops are typically fruits, while cool-season crops are root crops and salad greens. Optimum temperatures for cool-season crops range from highs of 70 to 75°F to lows of 40 to 45°F and soil temperatures of 40 to 45°F. Warm-season crops require highs of 75 to 85°F and lows of 50 to 60°F, and soil temperatures of 55 to 70°F. Warm-season crops tend to have deeper root systems than cool-season crops; they also need to be watered and fertilized often, as higher temperatures lead to faster evaporation and growth.

One factor that will certainly rein you and your garden bingeing in is available space. You may not be able to accommodate those 10 different varieties of peppers in your little veggie patch, so decisions will have to be made. How to choose among your dream plants, you ask? What to include and what to leave for next year? Here's how to make it easier: let your garden make the decision for you! The mere size of the garden will help you narrow your list, to include only what will produce the most, or is the most beautiful or the latest trend—the parameters are up to you, but your garden boundaries will dictate how far you can go. Voila! Control is back in your hands!

Take a seat with a few sheets of graph paper, a ruler, and a sharp pencil. Oh yes, and a good eraser too! Start with plotting out your garden on paper. Then make a list of all the edibles you enjoy along with those new ones you'd like to try. This is where you can let yourself go. Make the list as long as you'd like. Now, go back and prioritize the list in order of the volume you want to get from each plant. "How much zucchini do I want to bring into the kitchen each week? How many cucumbers will I want to harvest for slicing and pickling later in the season?"

TOOLS OF THE TRADE

Start bringing your gardening dreams to life by putting it down on paper. Don't be afraid—this is the first step to making your garden real. Although there are many free and fee-based online tools to help concretize your plan, here are two things that you may already have around the house.

Pencil 'n' paper. Graph paper, that is. This is the simplest method and one that I still use. Take a piece of graph paper and scale the drawing to best suit the size of your garden. Even if your garden is large, a scale of 1 square equaling 1 foot should allow you to fit the whole garden on the sheet. You can increase the scale if your garden is smaller.

Excel spreadsheet software. Many of you may have this spreadsheet software on your desktop or laptop. It's simple to turn this software into an easy garden design program. Just think of it as a big sheet of graph paper. Set the grid to show and adjust the size of the cells to squares. Use the border tool to draw the garden borders or raised beds, and then just scale the garden as you would on graph paper.

Another strategy is to consider how rare or expensive a certain edible on your list is in the market. Is it easier to pick up the Italian flat leaf parsley at the farmers' market and save the space to grow that less common variety of Asian greens you love but can never find? Honing your list this way will help you create the most valuable garden possible.

Now that you've got your list, it's time to fit it all into your space plan. But first, you will have to know all there is to know about the plants on your list, not only to make sure you're spacing correctly but to ensure you're siting the plant within your garden correctly as to exposure, microclimates, water needs, etc.—and putting those that need the same things together.

Plan for Raised Beds

Raised bed gardening has many advantages, so you'll probably want to sketch in a few. Here's why I'm so crazy about gardening in raised beds and containers.

Better drainage. Growing plants in raised beds is a logical choice for gardeners with heavy, poorly draining soils. Raised beds permit plant roots to develop in soil held above waterlogged or compacted zones, providing a better environment for root growth. As beds are built up, compost or other forms of organic matter may be incorporated, further improving soil structure, drainage, and nutrient-holding capacity.

Higher yields. Better root growth from improved soils leads to higher yields from your edibles. Also, intensive planting in raised beds means more plants can be grown in a smaller area than with conventional row-cropping techniques. No space is wasted between rows.

Expanded growing season. Better drainage speeds soil warming and allows earlier spring planting. In wet seasons, soil dries out faster, permitting planting to proceed between rains.

Eased maintenance. Because plants are growing above the level of footpaths, less stooping is required for weeding, watering, and other chores. Intensively planted raised beds (the strategy I prefer) provide dense foliage cover, shading out weeds.

Perhaps most important, raised beds make gardening possible on sites where growing plants would otherwise

COOL- AND WARM-SEASON EDIBLES

Cool. Agretti, artichokes, arugula, Asian greens, aspara- gus, beets, broccoli, Brussels sprouts, cabbage, carrots, cauliflower, celery, chard, cilantro, dill, fava beans, French tarragon, garlic, kale, leeks, lettuce, onions, pars- nips, peas, potatoes, radicchio, rhubarb, turnips.

Warm. Amaranth, basil, beans, corn, cucumber, drag- onfruit, edamame, eggplant, fenugreek, okra, peppers, strawberries, tomatillos, tomatoes, watermelon, zucchini.

Year-round perennials. Chives, fennel, oregano, thyme.

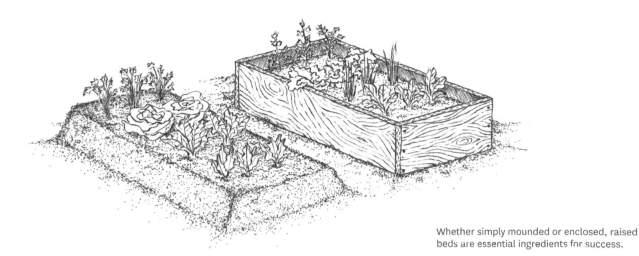

Whether simply mounded or enclosed, raised beds are essential ingredients for success.

be impossible (rooftop gardens, gardens on top of solid rock) or very challenging (gardens on slopes). Raised beds are very simple to build. Still, some of you may be interested in buying kits. Whichever route you choose, here are a few key elements to keep in mind.

Rooting depth = depth of raised bed. If this is important to know when you're planting into the ground (and it is!), it's even more important when you're growing in raised beds (and containers as well). My recommendation: if the native soil immediately below your raised bed site is unworkable or otherwise impaired, make sure you build your beds deep enough to allow you to grow the widest range of edibles possible (16 to 24 inches) and establish and maintain a healthy soil food web.

COLD HARDY AND SEMI-HARDY EDIBLES

We talk about cool-season crops when planting for the fall or early spring, but did you know that we could break down the category of cool-season crops further into two subcategories? This factoid will be especially helpful for the colder climate zones in the inland valleys.

Cold hardy. Tolerates minimum temperature of 40°F and short subfreezing conditions. Examples: asparagus, broccoli, Brussels sprouts, cabbage, chives, garlic, kale, leeks, onions, peas, rhubarb, turnips.

Semi-hardy. Tolerates minimum temperature of 40 to 45° and just a few hours of subfreezing conditions. Examples: beets, carrots, cauliflower, celery, chard, lettuce, parsnips, potatoes, and hardy herbs like dill, oregano, and thyme.

Raised bed width. For ease of use and to make sure you don't have to walk on your soil, causing compaction, make the beds a width that allows all gardeners who will be tending the beds to access the middle of the beds comfortably. That usually means a width of about 4 feet.

Materials. There are many options here. I've used redwood, cedar, urbanite (broken recycled concrete), and cement ash block. All work well and, of course, if you repurpose or reuse any of these materials, even better! The cedar and redwood (even unsealed) will last a good 5 to 10 years (depending on site/usage), which is a very acceptable life span.

Do not use pressure treated lumber. Even though there have been changes in the pressure treatment process, I still won't use it and, therefore, cannot recommend it to you. Do your own research. I'm sure you'll come to the same conclusion. After all, you've gone to all this trouble to keep your food source as pristine as possible, why risk chemicals leaching into your soil from your building materials?

Pest control. Take care to add one important element to the bottom of your beds: heavy-duty hardware cloth or gopher wire. Believe me, this extra step will save you much grief. This barrier method is the *only* thing that stopped gopher invasion in my school garden beds! For a time, at least: those buggers will eventually work their way through the barrier as it degrades, so expect to replace it every 5 to 6 years or so. Also, as you are designing your beds, consider adding a mechanism to support a removable hoop house around your bed. By changing out the screening material, you can use your hoop house for all sorts of needs beyond pest control, like sun, wind, and frost protection. My favorite mechanism is to attach brackets to the insides of the bed into which you can

KNOW WHAT YOU GROW!

> When researching any plants that are new to you, use Internet searches like "how to grow [name of plant]" but also add the words "cooperative extension [the name of your geographic location]." This will return only a list of articles from your local cooperative extension university, guaranteeing you are getting research-based advice.

easily slip bendable PVC pipes to form the hoop structure (see March's Skill Set). Hoop houses are essential players in pest protection and growing season extension.

Seedling Transplants

Now let's talk about your options for getting your hands on the stars of your garden: plant material. Yes, you have options! Seedling transplants will give your vegetable garden a small head start, and you do have choices when it comes to sourcing these transplants. We are all familiar with our local plant purveyors—everything from that small, sometimes family-owned neighborhood nursery to those big box stores. I urge you to vote with your wallet, choosing to support the nursery that has the most knowledgeable staff, cares for their plants sustainably and organically, and is a treat to visit (clean, well organized). To me, the most interesting nurseries are those that carry interesting, more exotic edibles that will help me broaden my gardening and culinary experience.

If you are a beginner who is a bit intimidated by starting from seeds, using transplants from a nursery is a great way to reduce your chances of failure and beat the clock, especially if you have a shorter growing season. I have a few tips to arm yourself with before you walk into that nursery.

Quality of nursery. Take a quick assessment walk through the nursery or plant department. Look to see that the majority of the plants seem healthy and well cared for.

Plant foliage. Evaluate the condition of your specific plant. Are the leaves green, shiny, and lush? Steer clear of any plants that are wilting or yellowing, as stressed plants may not recover once you plant them, regardless of how much care you take.

Insects and disease. Inspect closely for signs of insects or disease. Check both sides of the leaves, the stem, and the potting soil. Signs can include blackened areas, holes, spots, mushy areas, stickiness, and distortions. If any of these signs are present, pass the plant up. You don't want to bring any disease or pest into your garden on a new transplant if you can avoid it.

Root system. Don't forget the roots! If the plant is severely pot-bound, and the roots are growing out of the bottom of the pots or encircling the root ball, the plant may be stressed and take time to recover. If there aren't any exposed roots, and the plant lifts out easily (yes, you can do this), it was probably recently repotted and could use more time to become garden-worthy *and* worth the increased price that the nursery is charging for the larger-sized pot; in this case, it is better to select a plant in a smaller pot that has grown into its space. And remember to assess the health of the roots. In addition to avoiding severely pot-bound roots, avoid roots that look waterlogged or have any degree of rot. Roots should be light in color, and the root ball should have some plump, well-developed roots in addition to a web of smaller roots.

Weeds. Weeds in the pot are competing with the plant for nutrients. They also signal neglect by the nursery staff.

Buds vs flowers. Plants in bud will transplant and perform better than plants in flower (or worse yet, in fruit). If you can't resist buying that veggie with fruit setting, remove any fruit *and* flowers before putting it in your garden, so that the plant can focus its energy on establishing its root system in its new home rather than developing fruit. There's plenty of time for that after the plant has formed a great foundation of a solid root system, leaves, and stem.

Homeward Bound

Ok, you've carefully selected your nursery plants. Now it's time to get them into your garden. To help you get your plants off to a good start in their new home, here is my guide to proper transplanting techniques:

1. Make sure the plant is not dry. Water the plant so that the root ball is moist (not soggy) before transplanting.

2. Dig a hole that is about twice the width of the plant's container, but no deeper than the plant's root ball. There are exceptions to this. Tomatoes and tomatillos, for example, should be planted deeper than the typical veggie. Take into consideration the texture of the soil. If you have a very light or sandy soil, expect that the plant will sink a bit after being watered in.

3. Tap the sides of larger containers firmly with a trowel or lay the container gently on its side and press firmly along the sides, turning the container to gently loosen the root ball uniformly. With smaller containers, you can simply squeeze the pot to separate the root ball from the sides of the container. Remove the plant from the container by gently tipping the pot into your free hand, making sure to protect the stem from breakage. Avoid pulling on the trunk or stem of these smaller transplants.

4. "Tickling the toes" is how I refer to preparing the root ball when teaching kids how to transplant, and they never forget to do this. With any plant except for very young transplants, gently loosen the bottom of the root ball. With older plants whose roots are circling the bottom of the root ball, you may have to make vertical cuts to score the root ball and loosen roots. This encourages the roots to venture out into the new soil, instead of continuing to encircle the root ball, potentially strangling the plant.

5. Mix your organic materials (compost, castings, fertilizer) with the soil you removed when digging the hole. Evenly distribute soil around the new plant. Wait until your veggie seedling is where you want it (for the most part level with surrounding soil—except for tomatoes and tomatillos, which prefer a deeper planting) before gently pressing the soil so that the root ball comes into contact with new soil completely, without any large air gaps or spaces where water can collect. Be careful not to compact soil, however; that will have the opposite effect of squeezing out all air channels around the plant.

6. Water the plant thoroughly.

Bonus tip. Add a 2- to 3-inch layer of mulch. For best results, use your hands to spread the mulch and avoid layering mulch too thickly, as it can affect plant health. Don't allow mulch to make direct contact with the plants: form a ring 2 to 3 inches around plants instead. This will help avoid disease problems. When finished, water down the mulch to give it moisture and help it settle into place. Organic mulch options: leaf mulch, wood mulch, compost, straw, pine needles (slow to decompose, good way to acidify soil over time).

Seed Starting

As your skill set grows with handling transplants, you may become excited by the seemingly endless possibilities offered by growing your edibles yourself, from seed. This gives you access to varieties of veggies that are hard to find commercially—perhaps that unique turnip your great-grandmother grew decades ago! But as with any new thing, we need to learn a bit first before we put that order in to the seed house.

Certain environmental conditions need to be met in order to trigger seed germination. Generally, you'll achieve better germination if soil temperature is consistently at 70°F; some seeds germinate best at 80 to 85°F. Seeds also need consistent moisture, to soften their seed coats—but moist, not wet, just like a wrung-out sponge. Moisten your soil mix thoroughly and evenly before sowing (see January for my own seed-starting mix recipe). **TIP** To help keep soil from drying out, drape a sheet of plastic wrap on top of newly sown seeds. Check on moistness every day, and if seeds are starting to sprout, remove plastic.

Most seeds do not need light to germinate, but once the seeds begin to sprout above the soil and develop their first true leaves, they need a light source! A sunny south-facing window will do if you don't have a small greenhouse to work with. Grow lights can help too. If your seedlings are leggy, it probably means they're not getting enough light. Seedlings will also need a weak fertilizer to grow vigorously (a diluted compost tea is good). If you added compost to your seedling soil mix, you can delay the need for fertilizer a bit longer.

The correct timing of seed sowing is a critically important factor in successful indoor seed starting. In winter months, it's very easy to get itchy to start growing, and some gardeners sow seeds too soon. Seedlings that are held indoors too long tend to perform poorly once they are transplanted into the garden. Most seeds should be sown 4 to 12 weeks (depending on the particular veggie's germination rate) prior to transplanting into the garden (after your last frost date). Patience, the gardener says, is a virtue!

The time it takes for seedlings to be ready for transplanting outdoors will vary. Once the seeds have germinated, you will see two seed leaves or cotyledons. Eventually, these seed leaves will wither. Next, true leaves will form. These true leaves look like the plant's typical leaves. Transplant the seedlings to individual containers once the first set of true leaves appear. Included in the time it takes before the seedlings should be transplanted is a hardening off period of 1½ to 2 weeks.

TIP Some vegetables (beets, carrots, parsnips, turnips) don't like to be transplanted. They're cool-season vegetables, so you can direct sow them pretty early anyway. Crops like beans, corn, and peas are also pretty finicky about transplanting and grow better when you direct sow.

Your Garden's Diary

I hope gardening will become something that will remain a part of your life forever—and forever can be a long, long time. I don't know about you, but remembering even the previous year—what I planted, complete with varietal names; what problems cropped up and how I solved them—became a bit challenging as my garden and my experiences grew. I finally found an old-fashioned tool that helped me tremendously: the garden journal. Simple, really. It can be anything from an old notebook that you have lying around (I like a three-ring binder myself) or a beautiful old bound journal that you want to make a keepsake of, perhaps to hand down to the next generation of gardeners in your family. For those of you that are more high-tech, you can even use your tablet or smartphone (that's what my garden managers use out in the field).

Whatever form it takes, the secret to keeping any good garden journal is discipline and organization. The discipline is training yourself to take the time to do it and do it consistently. It should be something that you keep in your gardening tool kit, right along with your trowel. I usually remain in the garden while I make my notes, so that I can stroll back through to make sure I don't forget anything. It is the last thing I do before I leave the garden.

Garden journaling will not only help you avoid making the same mistake twice (as long as you also take the time to review it in subsequent years), it can also end up being a very sweet scrapbook of gardening through the years with your friends and family. Well worth the effort on so many levels!

Organizing your journal is important. Making it easy to reference and track information is vital to making it easy to use. Here's how I organize mine.

Garden plot plan. My journal opens with a simple sketched-out representation of my future garden. Because I use a three-ring binder, I can easily slip a piece of graph paper into it. I note every detail, in pencil, so changes are easy! Remember to make any notes about changes in the environment since the season before— was a tree removed or trimmed, did a wall or fence go up—anything that would change the exposure or microclimate.

Prepare site for planting. This is a to-do list, really. Listing the soil prep or irrigation repairs that need to be done will create a shopping list, too: amendments, fertilizers, pest control. Anything to be ready for planting day!

Early indoor seed starting. I use a greenhouse, but even if you're just using your kitchen window sill, good records of this activity will come in handy. I list the seed type (I note the seed house, too), variety, date planted, date germinated, date potted up, first date of hardening off, and date transplanted into garden.

Direct sowing/planting/growing/harvesting record. I keep a record of the seeds once they are planted by tracking the seed type, variety, where purchased (if nursery stock), date germinated, date of first and last harvest, and other notes about the plant.

Fertilizer, pest and disease control, and weather. Recording the application of fertilizer and pest and

HOW TO TAKE YOUR SOIL'S TEMPERATURE

Use a soil thermometer to track the temperature of the soil in your vegetable garden. Insert the thermometer probe to the depth you will sow seeds (1 to 2 inches). Test the temperature in the morning. When the soil temperature reaches a consistent reading for at least 3 consecutive days, you can use the table on soil temperature ranges to see what you can plant.

VEGETABLE	SOIL TEMP. RANGE (°F)
asparagus	60 to 85
beans	60 to 85
beets	50 to 85
cabbage	45 to 95
carrots	45 to 85
cauliflower	45 to 85
celery	60 to 70
chard	50 to 85
corn	60 to 95
cucumber	60 to 95
eggplant	75 to 90
lettuce	40 to 80
okra	70 to 95
onions	50 to 95
parsnips	50 to 70
peas	40 to 75
peppers	65 to 95
tomatoes	70 to 95
turnips	60 to 105
watermelon	70 to 95
zucchini	70 to 95

HOW TO TAKE BETTER PHOTOS OF YOUR GARDEN

Watching professional photographers at work in many of my gardens has shown me that a few things are must-dos if you are to achieve the kind of photos your garden deserves.

Neat and tidy. Make sure you have done a good, thorough cleanup in your garden, removing spent flowers, diseased leaves . . . anything that you wouldn't want anyone to see.

Let there be just a little light. The best time to shoot a garden is when the sun is not at its brightest—either in the early morning or on an overcast day with calm winds. Bright, full sun is the worst lighting for taking garden photos; the harsh light doesn't allow colors, textures, and other details to shine through.

Wet and wild. Watered soil looks better than dry soil to the camera (and nothing's more beautiful than the shimmer of droplets on your veggies), so give soil a good watering before you photograph.

Frame your subject. Close-ups of the perfect tomato or strawberry are great, but make sure you take your shots from many different perspectives to give your plants context and demonstrate the beauty of the whole garden, not just the bit players (as lovely as they may be).

Use the lines in the landscape (e.g., a border, hedge, or raised beds) to add depth to your photo. Any linear structure or pattern will do. This creates a photo of your garden that looks three-dimensional instead of flat.

disease controls helps keep you from accidentally over-using any of these, which can be detrimental to the plant and environment. Noting weather patterns also helps us draw correlations between weather and pest and disease issues. Referring back to this data the following year can help you anticipate problems before they develop.

Likes and dislikes, next year's dos and don'ts. I like to include this section to note specifics about what grew well, what didn't, and what I'd like to try again (or not) next year. This is also where I note varieties that I come across or read about—things I'd like to include in next season's garden. I take a lot of garden photos, too. Some I'll paste onto these pages: strange bugs, odd diseases, and, of course, just photos as evidence of how beautiful the garden was.

GET PLANTING

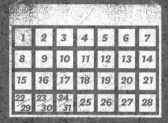

·JANUARY·

NEW BEGINNINGS AND OLD FRIENDS

In the South Coast, most of us haven't skipped a beat in our gardens and, with a few precautions, even inland valley gardeners blissfully "grow on" from fall into winter. But wherever we are in SoCal, January is a time of new promise. We can't help it. Seed catalogs of all types (what one gardener I know calls "gardening porn") are starting to arrive. There they are, in all their glory—glossy, full-color images of our horticultural dreams. This is how gardeners ring in the new year! We close last year's gardening journal, full of success and, yes, failure, and open a new journal—one blank page after another, full of potential!

TO DO THIS MONTH

PLAN

- Organize and dream over your seed catalogs
- Review your garden journal for last year's notes on your favorite and not-so-favorite plants
- Inventory your seeds and check their age
- Clean (boiled linseed oil is a great natural cleaner), oil, and sharpen tools
- Check supplies—fertilizers and organic sprays (they degrade with age), gloves, plant markers—and replenish if necessary
- Collect materials to reuse for seed-starting pots: egg cartons, papertowel tubes, newspaper, Keurig cups, plastic lidded take-out containers
- Order new seeds

PREPARE AND MAINTAIN

- Prune grapes
- Be prepared for frost in the inland valleys—build hoop houses, replace fleece and straw mulch

SOW AND PLANT

- Start an herb garden on your kitchen countertop
- Grow a crop of microgreens or sprouts indoors

HARVEST

- arugula
- beets
- broccoli
- Brussels sprouts
- cabbage
- carrots
- cauliflower
- chard
- chives
- cilantro
- dill
- French tarragon
- kale
- leeks
- lettuce
- parsnips
- potatoes
- radicchio
- turnips

So Many Seeds, So Little Space

Getting carried away (and maybe a bit overwhelmed) by the countless wonderful seed catalogs is part of the fun at this time of year. But at some point, we all need to focus and narrow down our list to those plants that answer the question, "What do I want to grow (and eat) this spring?" We touched on this process in the garden planning chapter. Now we'll take a closer look.

Start deciding what the focus of your garden will be. Will it provide your kitchen with all the staples you use daily or weekly? Or will it provide your household's budding culinary star with rare, exciting ingredients? A Market Basket garden or a Michelin-Starred Chef garden? That's the question!

Of course, it doesn't have to be all of one or the other. There are ways to have a garden that saves you from last-minute dashes to the grocery store but also gives you a few taste adventures, too. Spend a few minutes considering what those "must-haves" are first and then fill in the remaining space with your more exotic selections (those edibles that you wouldn't find on your dinner plate every night but would definitely see at a restaurant).

How to tell what's trending with chefs? Since most gardeners also list cooking as a hobby, there is probably more than one "foodie" magazine in your house. Read them! Those are great resources, fresh glimpses into what the most talented chefs are cooking with these days. Like fashion, food trends go in and out too, so keep current!

Your seed catalogs can help with this as well. When reading about a plant that is new to you, look for the words "market grower" in the description. That's a sure sign you're reading about an up-and-coming culinary star ingredient! Consider also that most vegetables currently trending are heirlooms (their seed has been saved over multiple generations—at least 50 years), and most have played a distinct role in the cultural heritage of ethnic populations around the globe. If collecting and growing these special plants is something that you'd like to try, seek out older seed houses that specialize in heirloom seeds (see Resources). Become familiar with the many available varieties of your favorites. That's a great way to introduce an aesthetic or flavor experience that's brand new and still have your "old friends" in the garden again!

Know What You've Got

"Getting organized"—a very popular resolution at this time of year, but it's especially critical here. If you don't know what seeds you've got in hand already and what is viable, you'll either over- or under-order, and by the time you've figured it all out, your favorite seeds are sold out for that planting year!

The system I use to organize seed stock for our restaurant production garden makes taking inventory a snap. You'll need one of those plastic portable hanging file folder bins that you can buy at any office supply store (choose one that is opaque, as you want to shield your seeds from light), some manila folders with assorted tab positions, and some vinyl sheet protectors, the kind you'd use in a three-ring binder. Here's what you'll do:

- Mark the name of the veggie on each folder you'll be storing.
- Put the seed packets into a sheet protector (this is to keep them from spilling out everywhere in the bin).
- Use a paper clip to hold the packets together inside the

sheet protector with the oldest year on top. This way you'll be sure to use up your oldest seed first (remember: many seeds stay viable for more than one year).

- Go one step further and use hanging file holders to separate cool-season seeds from warm-season seeds.
- Store your bin in a cool, dry, dark place.

Don't throw out your seeds just because it's past the "packed for" or "sell by" date on the packet. Seeds remain viable for varying lengths of time—they aren't "dead" by New Year's Day the following year. The seeds of most SoCal edibles are good for 3 to 4 years. Exceptions on the short side (2 years) are corn, leeks, okra, and peppers; on the long side, cucumber (5 years) and lettuce (6 years). Keep in mind, though: the closer it is to the end of a given viability time period, the lower the germination rate becomes. You'll have to plant more seed to get more to germinate than you did when you first got them.

MY SUSTAINABLE SEED-STARTING MIX RECIPE

5 parts organic compost (your own is best, of course)

4 parts garden soil*

1 to 2 parts sand (coarse, sharp, or construction sand—not playground sand)

1 to 2 parts leaf mold if available (if you're not composting your leaves, you should start!)

1 part coconut coir fiber (available online and in many nurseries or big box stores)

* Buy a good organic brand in reputable store, or you can sterilize your own in your oven: in a metal baking sheet, spread no more than 4 inches of garden soil at a time. Cover tightly with aluminum foil. Preheat oven to 180 to 200°F. Place soil in oven. Use an instant-read thermometer to check when soil temperature reaches at least 180°F and keep it there for 30 minutes. Remove and cool.

SKILL SET

....

SKILL SET: HOW TO MAKE NEWSPAPER SEED POTS

....

MATERIALS

a sheet of newspaper (roughly 22 × 12 inches) for each pot you want to make

one 10- to 15-ounce can

your favorite seed-starting mix (see sidebar for my favorite)

waterproof tray

STEPS

1 Fold the sheet of newspaper lengthwise to create a strip. Press along the folded edge.

2 Set the can on its side at one end of the strip, with the base about 2 inches up from the cut edge. Roll the newspaper around the can to create a cylinder.

3 Starting at the outer seam, fold the free end of the cylinder inward. Make three more folds inward to create the base of the pot, pressing firmly to make the folds as flat as possible.

4 Slip the pot off of the can. Starting at the outer seam, fold the top ½ to 1 inch of the pot inward to create a sturdy rim.

5 Hold the pot with one hand, with some of your fingers on the bottom to keep it closed. Fill the finished pot to the top with moistened seed-starting mix and set it in the tray.

6 Repeat steps 1 through 5 to make as many "pots" as desired.

·FEBRUARY·

SPRING TRAINING

Although our gardening kin in colder climes are still dealing with freezes and snow banks, we lucky ones in SoCal are probably looking at mostly clear but chilly skies with some rain events—if we're lucky. Freezes are still possible in our inland valleys, but the odds are in our favor that it is time for us all to start preparing for our spring planting. Spring equinox is next month, and it's coming up fast and furious, so you'd better be ready. What to do to get you, your garden, and your tool shed ready for spring? That's what's "to do" this month.

TO DO THIS MONTH

PLAN

- Get into shape for spring—start a light exercise program like walking or biking, beginning and ending with a good stretching routine targeting those muscles we gardeners use most
- Organize your tool shed and potting bench, making sure all supplies are within reach and easy to find with gloved, dirty hands
- Order bare-root plants and starts—asparagus, garlic, grapes, onions, potatoes, strawberries

PREPARE AND MAINTAIN

- Continue to prune grapes
- Check for overwintering insects and fungal diseases
- Add compost, leaf mold, earthworm castings to soil
- Be prepared for frost in the inland valleys, ready to protect crops with hoop houses, cold frames, fleece, and straw mulch
- Check to make sure the fleece in your hoop house or cold frame is secure, with no holes, and the lid of the cold frame is intact

SOW AND PLANT

- Sow seed for cool-season crops but be ready to protect against a late frost
- Start sowing warm-season edibles indoors late in the month
- Plant any of the cool-season edibles or year-round perennials that can be harvested this month; they might have been growing in your garden since fall. If not, it's not too late!

HARVEST

- arugula
- beets
- broccoli
- Brussels sprouts
- cabbage
- carrots
- cauliflower
- celery
- chard
- chives
- cilantro
- dill
- French tarragon
- kale
- leeks
- lettuce
- parsnips
- peas
- potatoes
- radicchio
- strawberries
- thyme

Me, Myself, and I

First and foremost, you can't be a good (or happy) gardener if hurting, aching, huffing and puffing, or running off to get the nearest fit human to do the inevitable heavy lifting is part of your gardening reality. Folks, this is hard work. It's great exercise, but you need to prepare your body just as you would for any other form of exercise or sport you do.

Start walking. Not far, just a mile or so during the first couple of weeks. Gradually add distance and more challenging topography, and do this three or four times a week if possible. Walk somewhere that is a calm and peaceful setting for you. This should be as much a mental stress reducer as it is a physical exertion. Go to a local park, community garden, beach—any place that you'd like to be even if you weren't there to exercise.

You'll find that you'll look forward to your walk each day because it is a special destination for both your mind and body that will not only improve your physical readiness for gardening but your mental outlook as well. If you can't work your walks into your routine this month, no worries—it's never too late. Just start!

Like in any sport, the best coaches/trainers will tell you to warm up before you play! Gardening is no different. Your body needs a good 10 minutes of a slow stretch and muscle warm-up routine to help it avoid muscle strain and injury. You know where you're feeling muscles tightening, so start by doing slow stretches targeting those muscles. Here's a stretch that focuses on a common problem zone, the gluteus maximus, which gets shortened by overuse or long winter stints at the computer (designing your next dream garden, I'm sure).

GARDEN TOOL ERGONOMICS

Selecting the tool that fits and using it safely is an important part of healthy gardening.

Long-handled tools should be at least as tall or a bit taller than you are, so that you can stand up straight while using them.

Hoes or rakes. You should be standing perpendicular to where you want to work, extending the tool out to your side and pulling the tool in to your body. If you've selected a tool that fits, you'll avoid overextending, which can tire or strain your back.

Shovel. Hold the end of the shovel with both hands, putting your dominant hand on top of the other. Extend your arms all the way in front of you with the point of your shovel straight down. Drive the shovel into the ground as far as it will go with your foot. Pull back with your arms to your side, breaking up the ground. Slide your hand down the shaft near the head of the shovel while slowly bending with your knees, not your back (here's where those warm-up exercises come in handy). Slowly stand back up and toss the dirt close by so as not to overextend, which could hurt your back. Remember not to overdo, and pick up only about half of a shovel load to prevent strain on your back.

1. Sit on a garden bench or chair and cross one leg over the other, with the ankle on top of the other knee.

2. Sit up straight, squeezing your shoulder blades together.

3. Lean slightly forward into the stretch. Ahh! I can hear you all sighing from here!

And remember: you are what you eat. Growing your own food already makes you more aware of the nutritional value of the food your garden gives you. That's a great start! If you think your diet could use some improvement (and whose doesn't?), start by making sure you're using all the veggies you are growing. Research shows that more plants (than animals) on a plate is healthier for us.

The Bare Essentials

'Tis the season for planting bare-root trees and vines! Purchasing bare-root specimens is an affordable way to include the trees and vines of your dreams in your garden. Just as the term "bare-root" implies, the plants arrive naked, leafless, and dormant, with their roots free of soil. You can buy bare-root fruit trees, grape vines, caning berries, asparagus, and hops, among many ornamental shrubs and trees.

One of the advantages of planting bare-root stock, beyond the money savings, is that the roots can be easily inspected before you buy so you can select only healthy stock. If you are going through mail order, inspect the plants as soon as they arrive and return any that don't measure up.

Select plants that are fully dormant with no leaf or buds emerging. Make sure there is no obvious damage to the roots and that they seem well hydrated (the whole plant should feel heavy for its size). The root system should be balanced in formation, not one-sided, J-shaped, kinked, or girdled or circling near the crown, as if the plant was pot-bound. Plants should also smell good, not moldy or decayed. Some minor damage to branches can be accepted.

You should plan ahead and be ready to plant as soon as your bare-root specimens arrive. If for some reason you cannot, you must keep their root systems covered, well hydrated, and sheltered from harsh sun, freezing temperatures, and wind. Aside from the prescribed pre-planting soak that different bare-root plants may require, do not leave your plants sitting in water for extended periods of time—never more than 12 to 18 hours.

SKILL SET: HOW TO PLANT BARE-ROOT PLANTS

STEPS

1 Select a site that gives the plant the exposure it requires. Pay attention not only to sun exposure but wind and chill exposure as well.

2 The soil should be well draining and have a good amount of organic matter. Add compost, if in doubt. If you are dealing with heavy soils that have been compacted, some tilling in of compost will help improve fertility, tilth, and drainage. Do not plant into soil that drains poorly.

3 Dig a hole large enough and deep enough to accommodate the root system. Form a firm cone at the bottom of the hole tall enough to support the root system without burying or exposing the crown (look for the soil mark or bark color change caused by the soil level in its previous environment at the grower).

Mix some organic nitrogen fertilizer into the backfill soil using the recommendations on the package.

4 Spread the root system over and around the soil cone and backfill with the amended excavated soil. Press in firmly but do not compact. Remember that there will be settling, depending on the soil texture (sandy soil = plant settles lower after irrigation), so watering while backfilling may help you anticipate any adjustments that need to be made to correct height.

5 Grafted trees: Make sure the bud or graft union (easily identified by the bulge in the base of the trunk) is at least 1 inch above the soil. Face the crook of the budded or grafted union south, into the sun. This will make the crook self-shading, so that the face of the bud or graft union is protected from the damaging effects of direct sun.

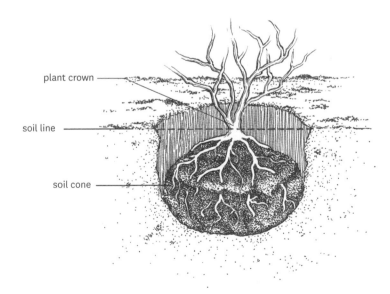

plant crown

soil line

soil cone

When planting bare-root plants, spread the root system over and around the soil cone.

·MARCH·

A "SHOULDER" SEASON

March is the sweet spot between winter and spring, with the equinox usually falling around the 20th of the month. It's the beginning of one of the year's two "shoulder" seasons, transitional periods which can last anywhere from a few weeks to over a month, while the climate finds its footing. As every seasoned gardener will attest, these annual shifts are further complicated by the changing weather patterns of the last decade, and they can now confound even the most experienced gardeners. The March shift in particular keeps us on our toes. It could quickly warm up—or seem to take forever to shake off the chill of winter. But that's what makes me love it.

TO DO THIS MONTH

PLAN

- Finalize your garden planting plan
- Be ready to reassess and adapt your plan to the fickle weather: there is still a chance of a late frost in the inland valleys, but on the coast we can experience warm early springs
- Look back in your journal notes for last spring's weather patterns (frost, rainfall, heat, cold), soil temperature readings (when did soil come up to 40°F?), and planting lists (your likes and dislikes, successes, failures)
- Research any plants on your planting list that are new to you

PREPARE AND MAINTAIN

- Prepare your garden journal for the new season
- Continue to add organic matter to soil
- Prune deciduous grapes early in the month (this is your last chance), in case a warm early spring triggers early budding
- Continue to be prepared for frosts (inland valleys)
- Check for overwintering insects and fungal diseases

SOW AND PLANT

- Plant out starts or transplants (for a jump start on the season): garlic, onion, and potato starts, winter lettuce, broccoli, cauliflower, celery, dill, fava beans, French tarragon, leeks, oregano, thyme
- Direct sow: arugula, Asian greens, beets, cabbage, carrots, chard, cilantro, kale, lettuce, peas, radicchio (inland valleys—be prepared to protect against late frost with cold frame or hoop house)

HARVEST

- arugula
- Asian greens
- asparagus
- broccoli
- Brussels sprouts
- cabbage
- carrots
- cauliflower

- celery
- chard
- chives
- cilantro
- dill
- fava beans
- fennel
- fenugreek

- French tarragon
- garlic
- kale
- leeks
- lettuce
- onions
- oregano
- parsnips

- peas
- potatoes
- radicchio
- strawberries
- thyme
- turnips

Remembering the Past

Remember the Old Farmer's Almanac? It was the reference many of our forebearers used to anticipate astronomical cycles (sun and moon), tides, and weather patterns, not just year to year but decade to decade, and it often meant the difference between success and ruin for farmers. These natural events are patterns that repeat themselves over the course of time, and in 1792, from the records of these natural cycles, the Almanac's first editor, Robert B. Thomas, developed a weirdly accurate secret formula that predicted the weather with 80% accuracy. The Old Farmer's Almanac is published to this day; my current edition, filled with the same folksy mixture of science and humor, always arrives when my seed catalogs do.

Before the Almanac, the only written reference our agrarian ancestors had to predict weather patterns were their own journals. Before written language, it was the storytellers of ancient societies that handed down their farming methods and records of weather patterns through folktales from generation to generation. Your gardening journal becomes your personal almanac, so be sure to keep it up to date year after year. You'll be a better gardener because of it.

One Foot in Winter, Another in Spring

Reviewing your journal notes from last year and keeping an eye on local weather forecasts—both will be necessary for successfully navigating this transitional period between winter and spring. This watchful waiting will allow you to make a solid judgment call about when it may be the proper time to plant the specific edibles on your list for spring.

JOURNALING TIPS

DIY. Yes, you can buy a journal, but it's just as easy to make your own—a simple three-ring binder and sheets of paper you can design on your computer with headings that will guide your journaling.

Track the things that are important. Keep seed-starting and transplant records, noting dates germinated/planted and varieties; sketches of garden plan and layout; soil management and soil temperature readings; weather conditions (including frost dates); pest and disease problems—and how you handled it all.

Add a reference guide. Make a section to include printouts of gardening articles, recipes, and pictures of your garden and others. It's a resource, a historical record, and inspiration for next season combined.

Think about tomorrow. Include notes of dreams for next season's garden as they come to you.

In coastal regions, temperatures can still reach lows of 35 to 40°F at night, but daytime temperatures have also been known to spike into the high 70s or more in years with warm springs. Even though USDA lists zone 9's last frost date as around mid-February, some inland valleys continue to run the risk of a light, late frost during cold springs. Gardeners in those areas need to be prepared to give their plants a bit of protection at night, so don't put your cold frames, hoop houses, or cloches away just yet.

Soil temperature is another crucial bit of data when determining when your conditions are perfect for planting. Refer back to the garden planning chapter for the soil temperature ranges required by specific edibles and instructions on taking your soil's temperature.

LIGHT FROST TO HARD FREEZE

Being prepared to effectively deal with the possibility of cold temperatures and even frost or freeze during the shoulder seasons is extremely important. But all freezes are not created equal; here are the different levels of freeze:

frost or light freeze	28 to 32°F
moderate freeze	24 to 28°F
hard or killing freeze	less than 24°F

SKILL SET

SKILL SET: HOW TO BUILD A HOOP HOUSE

A hoop house will help you extend your growing season through both shoulder seasons, between winter and spring, and between summer and fall. This hoop house is designed to fit over a raised bed that is 4 × 8 feet in size.

MATERIALS

six ½-inch PVC pipes cut at 8 feet
1½-inch bolts and wing nuts
cover material (fleece or landscape fabric)
cable ties and landscape pins (aka staples)

STEPS

1 Drill a hole every 2 feet in one PVC pipe section (this will form the stabilizing pipe that runs along the top of all others to keep the hoops in place).

2 Drill a hole every 4 feet in the remaining five pipes (in the middle of each pipe)

3 Lay out the five pipes along the length of your raised bed. Lay the stabilizing pipe along the middle of the other five pipes and match up each pipe so that the pipes all line up with the predrilled holes.

4 Insert the 1½-inch bolts into the predrilled holes and secure with the wing nuts. Tighten.

5 Place each pipe end on the inside of the raised bed, bending the pipes to form the hoop. Push the pipes down into the soil and level.

6 Wrap the frame with fleece (available in varying weights for frost protection) or landscape fabric (also available in varying degrees of weight for wind and sun protection). Secure the cover material to the frame using cables ties and to the soil using landscape pins.

Note: If you feel you need to secure the hoop house a bit more, you can insert 3-foot rebar posts into the soil where you are putting each PVC pipe, pounding them down into the ground and then inserting the end of the pipes into each rebar.

READY, SET, GROW

Now the real work begins, but you're ready! Your watchful waiting until weather patterns and soil temperatures became seasonally appropriate has paid off. You made adjustments in your plan, and your spring garden is off to a good, sound start. The best thing you can do for your garden now is to spend time in it. Take your morning coffee out to the yard, sit on a garden bench or perch on the edge of your raised bed, and look around. You'll be surprised how much you can notice in just five minutes! Do the same thing when you get home, and your garden will reward you with healthier growth and higher yields. It's a win-win.

TO DO THIS MONTH

PLAN

- Plan for your warm-season garden
- Develop your planting list and acquaint yourself with any plants that are new to you
- Monitor weather and soil temperature through the month to determine if it is time to move fully toward sowing warm-season plants in your area of SoCal

PREPARE AND MAINTAIN

- Pull weeds! It's spring for weeds too, so put this chore at the top of your list
- Clean birdbaths and bird and hummingbird feeders thoroughly
- Check for overwintering insects; as the temperature warms, both pest and disease activities will ramp up, so be prepared
- Fertilize your garlic, onions, and other starts
- Tend and pot up any warm-season seedlings started indoors previously
- Build raised beds and vertical plant supports, and buy containers

SOW AND PLANT

- Succession sow quick-maturing crops as the first plantings are nearing harvest; this is the best way to maximize your yield: arugula, Asian greens, chard, cilantro, kale, lettuce, radicchio
- Direct sow warm-season edibles if air/soil temperature is good, or start indoors: basil, beans, corn, cucumber, eggplant, peppers, tomatillos, tomatoes, watermelon, zucchini

HARVEST

- agretti
- amaranth
- artichokes
- arugula
- Asian greens
- asparagus
- basil
- beets
- broccoli

- cabbage
- carrots
- celery
- chard
- chives
- cilantro
- dill
- fava beans
- fennel

- fenugreek
- French tarragon
- garlic
- kale
- leeks
- lettuce
- onions
- oregano
- peas

- potatoes
- radicchio
- strawberries
- thyme
- turnips
- zucchini

Spring Is Here

Oh yes, we're well into spring and it's glorious. But this is no time to rest on your laurels. It's time to plan for the next temperature shift—the warm season. Your weather watching continues through this month as well, so that you'll be able to decide when to start planting your warm-season favorites. Another effect of increasing temperatures and longer days is faster growth (good) and more active pests and disease (not so good—as much as your chickens, if you have them, will appreciate the grubs and other new foraging opportunities), so your vigilance now is even more crucial.

The easiest way to spot pest trouble is by keeping your eye out for any discoloration or damage on leaves. Changes to leaves tell us a lot about the culprit and even lead us straight to it. Sort of like csi. Symptoms of fungal disease show up in the leaves as well. Identification is easy once you know the signs and understand the environmental conditions that lay out the welcome mat.

Fungal diseases can be hard to control once the spores are present. A general organic fungicide effectively treats powdery mildew, but blight is a different story. Tomatoes and potatoes are open to blight infection any time of the growing season, depending on the conditions, so frequent garden checks are a must. The most effective management strategy for late blight is to avoid sources of early season spores (which both potato tubers and tomatoes could harbor) now, in April. One important way to avoid introducing late blight on potatoes is to plant healthy certified seed potatoes. Many states where potato seed is produced have seed certification programs to ensure that the seed meets certain standards for disease levels. Keep in mind that certified seed is not a guarantee that late blight will not be present. Examine your seed and your tomato transplants carefully before you buy and plant them. In the case of potatoes, plant only sound, blemish-free tubers.

Chances are that fungal diseases, especially blight, will find you. But there are other things you can do to lessen your chances or reduce or control the outbreak:

- Make sure you're routinely adding plenty of organic matter to your soil—it's teeming with "good" fungi that can counteract the "bad" fungi.
- Clean, clean, clean! Blight can survive on living or dead plant tissue and in the soil or compost pile

FUNGAL DISEASE	SIGNS	FAVORED ENVIRONMENT
early blight	older leaves will be damaged first with target-like, ½-inch round spots, surrounded by a yellowing area	warm, moist
late blight	black lesions on leaves that turn brown and die	cool, humid
powdery mildew	grayish white powdery mat	moist, humid
septoria leaf spot	yellow lesions that later become round with gray centers and dark borders	warm, moist

for over a year, so practice good soil hygiene! Do a thorough end-of-season garden clean up, and bag and dispose of any remnants of diseased plants (do not compost!). Thoroughly clean your tools after working on an infected plant and at season's end (soak in 9 parts water to 1 part bleach, rinse well, and dry completely). If you are stepping on soil that you suspect might be infected, clean your shoes.

- Water only underneath the plants, not the leaves or fruit. Drip irrigation is preferable to watering with a hose, to reduce water splash. Don't overfertilize or overwater.

- Growing plants under an overhang or a clear plastic shelter can help prevent spores from being deposited on plants by wind and rain. But plants must be covered before infection has occurred. Do not cover the plants after they are infected, as it raises humidity and may worsen the problem.

- Remove diseased leaves or shoots immediately and all plants that are severely diseased. Bury them, or seal them in a plastic bag and take to a landfill. Do not compost diseased plants. If spores are present, they will survive in compost. So a *thorough* cleanup between seasons is important.

- Use resistant varieties when available. Planting resistant varieties of potatoes and tomatoes will slow down (but not prevent) blight.

- Remove all last year's tomato or potato debris to prevent carryover of disease.

- Destroy any volunteer potato or tomato plants in the garden. Destroy any nightshade weeds along fencerows. Nightshade is related to tomato and potato and is also a good host for blight.

- Grow tomatoes in a warm, dry, sunny area. If you have

had blight previously, make sure to practice good crop rotation.

- Grow tomatoes on raised beds with well-spaced trellises or in containers off the ground. Tomatoes grown on balconies or rooftops rarely develop late blight, probably because the environment is warmer and drier.

Growing Up

I'm used to small spaces. As a specialist in urban edible gardening, I'm quite happy designing gardens that take advantage of every single inch of growing space, horizontal and vertical. As a biointensive production grower, I'm equally adept at designing my planting plans to achieve the highest yields out of small spaces. In addition to following the biointensive method, this means utilizing a couple of different strategies.

A very effective way to maximize the productivity of your growing space is to grow vertically on supports like trellises, pergolas, teepees, obelisks, and arches made from materials like wood, bamboo, rebar, wire fencing, or plastic. Many of these vertical systems are available for purchase; they are also fairly easy to build yourself.

Many people who visit my urban farm are surprised by some of the plants I grow on vertical supports. The twining vines (beans, cucumber, peas, vining squashes) are the easiest to grow vertically, as they'll do all the climbing themselves via their tendrils. But that doesn't stop me from growing other tall plants vertically—I just tie them manually to the support. If it runs (fava beans, caning berries, even melons), I can grow it up. I grow indeterminate tomatoes up a 7-foot arch.

Growing vertically not only increases a garden's

productivity but also provides two other equally import-ant functions: design elements and shading mechanisms for tender plants. Upright structures bring depth and texture to an edible garden, and their varying shapes, heights, and even colors create boundaries and define space within a garden. Placed strategically, vertical supports can also provide season-extending shelter for lettuce and other sensitive edibles, which is very helpful when you're looking forward to enjoying delicate greens all through the summer.

Vertical garden support structures

Succession Planting

Succession planting is another tool I use to increase productivity and yield, especially when space is limited. Not only are you using space efficiently, but you're making the most out of the time you have. There are several ways you can use this technique:

- Two or more edibles in succession, for example when a cool-season crop is followed by a planting of a warm-season crop.

- Single edible in succession. This works especially well with faster-maturing crops like greens, planted at staggered timings. I plant leafing lettuces and greens every 7 days.
- Two or more crops simultaneously. For example, during the warmer months, I plant Nero di Toscana kale, which can get very tall, with arugula at its feet. As the kale grows, it will shade the more tender arugula from the midday sun.

SKILL SET

SKILL SET: DIY ARCH

You can easily build simple vertical supports that won't cost a lot but will make a big impression in your garden. This project is a garden arch made from rebar mesh, which is available at any big box hardware store. It has a distinctively rustic, almost industrial look that is simple and disappears when covered with plant material. Here's how to make it.

MATERIALS

two rebar mesh panels, 4 × 7 feet
four 4-foot rebar posts
rebar wire

STEPS

1 Lay the panels end to end so that the panels overlap by 1 foot.

2 Use the rebar wire to tie the overlap of the panels together snuggly.

3 Stand on the part of the panels that overlapped and bend each side of the panels up, forming an arch.

4 Place the mesh arch where you want it in the garden and drive the four 4-foot rebar posts (one on each side of each panel) securely into the ground. Tie the panels tightly to the rebar posts with wire.

EDIBLE LANDSCAPES, "FWB"

When I began designing edible landscapes, the Great Recession was at its worst and people from every walk of life were struggling to cope with a new reality. They wanted to get back to basics, keep closer to home, regain control over at least a small part of their lives. For some, a garden provided their families with economic relief. For others, it was a found bit of quiet sanity in the midst of the insanity swirling around them. They longed to turn even their front yards into productive spaces that could help sustain their family while still looking beautiful to their neighbors—but how to do that? "Edible landscapes," I cried, "that's how!"

TO DO THIS MONTH

PLAN

- Finalize your warm-season planting list and acquaint yourself with any plants that are new to you
- Follow a biointensive planting strategy, so you'll spend much less time weeding once the garden fills in
- Monitor weather and soil temperature to determine if it is time to move fully toward sowing warm-season plants in your area of SoCal

PREPARE AND MAINTAIN

- Keep your birdbaths and bird and hummingbird feeders filled and cleaned
- Keep up with insects and disease as the weather continues to warm
- Stay on top of your weeding!
- Watch your greens for leaf color change (light green to yellow foliage on older leaves first) and loss of vigor: it may be time to fertilize with
- nitrogen (good organic sources are blood meal, fish meal, bat guano, or cottonseed meal)
- Adjust your irrigation timer to suit the season, and monitor your drip irrigation to make sure everything is working properly
- Add micro-lines and adjust or relocate micro-sprayers to suit plant growth, if needed

SOW AND PLANT

- Succession sow quick-maturing crops as the first plantings are nearing harvest; this is the best way to maximize your yield: arugula, Asian greens, chard, cilantro, kale, lettuce
- Continue to direct sow warm-season edibles: basil, beans, corn, cucumber, eggplant, peppers, tomatillos, tomatoes, watermelon, zucchini
- Plant culinary herbs: cilantro, dill, fennel, French tarragon, oregano, thyme

HARVEST

- agretti
- amaranth
- artichokes
- arugula
- Asian greens
- asparagus
- basil
- beans
- carrots
- chard
- chives
- cilantro
- fava beans
- fenugreek
- French tarragon
- garlic
- kale
- lettuce
- okra
- onions
- oregano
- peas
- potatoes
- rhubarb
- strawberries
- thyme
- tomatillos
- tomatoes
- watermelon
- zucchini

The Incredible Edible Landscape

Edible landscaping is the use of food-producing plants in the constructed landscape, principally the residential landscape. Edible landscapes combine fruit and nut trees, berry bushes, vegetables, herbs, edible flowers, and ornamental plants into aesthetically pleasing designs (not necessarily row by row!) that are the perfect mixture of beauty and utility. Their additional health and economic benefits are the cherry on top.

Edible landscaping is as old as gardening itself. Ancient Persian gardens combined both edible and ornamental plants. Medieval monastic gardens included fruits, vegetables, flowers, and medicinal herbs. Plans for 19th-century English suburban yards, which modeled themselves after country estates, often included edible fruits and berries. But in this country, the practice of including edible components in home landscapes was largely lost to shade trees, lawns, and foundation plantings. In the past three decades, however, there has been a resurgence of interest in edible landscaping, thanks to the work of early pioneers such as Rosalind Creasy.

Like all plants used in the landscape, edible plants grow best in certain conditions. Here are four points to keep in mind when thinking about using this landscaping approach:

1. Exposure. Many (but not all) fruits and vegetables do best where they receive at least 6 hours and as much as 8 hours of full direct sunlight a day.

2. Soil texture. As we learned in the Gardening 101, most edibles do better in a light, loamy, well-draining soil that is rich in organic material.

3. Soil pH. Again, most edibles thrive in a soil pH of 6.5 to 7.5 (slightly acid to neutral)

ELEMENTS OF GOOD DESIGN

Some basic design elements apply to any landscape:

Unity. Consistency and repetition create unity. Repeat like elements (plants, groups of plants ,or décor) throughout the landscape, and all the elements fits together as a whole.

Simplicity. Pick two or three colors and repeat them throughout the garden or landscape.

Balance. A sense of equality, often achieved through symmetry.

Color. Use colors to create moods, movement, and create illusions of space (bright colors advance toward you; cool colors recede). Using coarse-textured, dark plants in the front and finely textured and light-colored plants in the back creates depth in the landscape. Remember that complementary colors (located opposite each other on the color wheel) create a more lively, exciting landscape. Analogous colors (directly beside a color) create a sense of harmony and, in the case of the cool colors, a sense of calm.

4. Water requirements. Make sure the plants on your list have like irrigation needs. Most edibles tend to be in the thirstier range, in line with roses and turfgrass.

So how do you start? No need to rip out your entire existing landscape. As long as your soil, exposure, and the rest of the existing plant material is compatible with edibles, you can start simply. Consider beginning with a one-for-one substitution as plants age out or fail. Where you might have planted a shade tree, plant a fruit tree. Where you need a deciduous shrub, plant a currant or blueberry bush. Where you have always had coreopsis, plant nasturtiums or other edible flowers. Even your A to Z vegetables have edible flowers (be sure to remove the pistil and stamens, which can taste bitter): arugula, broccoli, chives, cucumber, fava beans, oregano, peas, zucchini. Edible plants come in nearly all shapes and sizes and can perform the same role in the landscape as ornamental plants. Just be sure to research all the plants in your planned edible landscape, edibles and non-edibles alike, so that your choices allow the whole landscape to work together. In other words, make sure you're not putting a drought-tolerant plant next to a watermelon.

Designing an Edible Landscape

Designing a landscape that includes edibles involves the same design principles as a traditional landscape. Before you begin, think about the goals for your garden. Are you less interested in a large production edible garden and more interested in the beautiful aesthetics of including edibles in your ornamental landscape—or vice versa? If your goal to produce enough food for your family, then you'll approach your design from that perspective, integrating the design logistics that are required for a production garden (accessibility, yield, raised beds, etc.)

SKILL SET: AN EDIBLE BOUQUET FOR MOTHER'S DAY

Take advantage of the myriad shapes, colors, and textures of the edibles in your garden to create a gorgeous and unexpected floral centerpiece for Mom!

Take a walk through your landscape to see what's on offer. Look for unusual structures, colors, and textures— anything that would be a surprise. Think artichokes, sprigs of cherry tomatoes, tender pea shoots with tendrils, herbs and aromatics like dill, fennel, oregano, thyme (any of these in flower are a special feature), blossoms of any edible that has bolted, flowering onions, beautiful kale in different colors and textures. Immature fruit emerging from flowers (like beans, eggplant, fava beans, peas) are especially exquisite!

Don't forget the bottom of the vase. I always use clear vases, as I love to include nuts or bright cranberries (I freeze them), hard-skinned veggies (think root veggies like carrots, parsnips, turnips), or citrus fruits with thick rinds in the water. To showcase the underwater display even more, you can even slice the veggies. You'll have to change the water every couple of days to keep the water clear and clean and replace the sliced veggies every few days.

Decide what size vase you want to use and cut flower stems (at 45° angle) accordingly. Immediately place stems in a bucket of cool water.

Start arranging the flowers in the vase, remembering the design principles from this section as you do. What flowers or veggies are you going to showcase or feature in your design? Build the arrangement around them. You may need to support the heavier, bulkier veggies or fruits with bamboo skewers or floral wire. Enjoy!

·JUNE·

GRAY AND GLOOM

There are dues to be paid for living in paradise. Just when the spring garden is hitting its stride, it's blindsided by the infamous June Gloom, as it's come to be called by everyone from meteorologists to confounded tourists. It's the SoCal gardener's annual headache and, sometimes, heartache—the weather phenomenon that can bring on early blight, powdery mildew, and aphids. In some years, June Gloom lasts from May Gray into No-Sky July and, finally, Fogust. As for me, I enjoy this time of year: it delays the inevitable heat and humidity of summer. So stand tall in the fog, face down the slugs and snails, my friends—just stay calm and garden on.

TO DO THIS MONTH

PLAN

- Keep up your notes in your journal and check back—was your cool-season growing prolonged last year because of a gloomy June?
- Continue to monitor weather and soil temperature through the month to determine if you can move fully toward sowing warm-season plants in your area of SoCal

SOW AND PLANT

- Continue to succession sow quick-maturing crops, to maximize yield: arugula, Asian greens, chard, kale
- Continue to direct sow and plant warm-season edibles: basil, beans, corn, cucumber, eggplant, peppers, tomatillos, tomatoes, watermelon, zucchini

PREPARE AND MAINTAIN

- Attract pollinators by planting colorful edible flowers, the "lipstick" in the edible garden
- Keep a sharp lookout for pests and disease as the gloom lifts and the temperature warms
- Pull weeds!
- Continue to monitor your plants' need for additional nitrogen fertilizer, especially if you're pushing your leafy greens hard by planting intensely or harvesting often
- Taper off the nitrogen fertilizer and side-dress with an organic phosphorus fertilizer to promote bloom and fruit set, once fruiting plants are established and blooms appear
- Be water-wise: monitor your drip irrigation system and timer to suit the weather

HARVEST

- agretti
- amaranth
- artichokes
- arugula
- Asian greens
- basil
- beans
- chard
- chives
- corn
- cucumber
- edamame
- eggplant
- fava beans
- fenugreek
- French tarragon
- garlic
- kale
- okra
- oregano
- peas
- peppers
- rhubarb
- strawberries
- thyme
- tomatillos
- tomatoes
- watermelon
- zucchini

Changing Weather, Changing Plans

As any gardener knows, weather doesn't always cooperate with us. It's the good gardener that knows to side step, move around, and adjust to the problem. We don't quit. We adapt. Learn to watch the weather patterns as you've been doing throughout the year to be able to predict the likelihood of problems they bring and be ready for them.

Aphids, for example, multiply in cool temperatures followed quickly by warm temperatures, much like the June Gloom pattern of cool mornings under cloud cover giving way to sunny warm afternoons. (I find taking a damp paper towel and wiping them off to be effective.) And damp, humid weather with moderate temperatures promotes fungal diseases. Fungi play a large role in our soil systems and, as decomposers, they play a major role in cycling carbon and other elements. As good as that sounds, fungus can also be devastating to our plants, causing a host of diseases. Understanding how easily the spores can be spread—via wind, rain, irrigation, contaminated tools, shoes and hands—will better prepare you to contain the infection.

Early blight happens quickly under warm, humid conditions just like what SoCal experiences in a June Gloom pattern. Leaf lesions will be seen on older leaves first, with round spots of about ½ inch in diameter, resembling a "target-like" pattern, surrounded by a yellowing area. On the fruit the lesions look dry, with the same "target-like" pattern; they are seen most often on the stem end of the fruit.

Late blight, the same disease that lead to the Irish Potato Famine in the 1840s, is caused by a fungal-like pathogen, *Phytophthora infestans*, that survives from one season to the next in infected potato tubers and tomato transplants as well as dead potato and tomato vines. This very destructive and infectious organism can produce millions of spores under unseasonably cool, wet weather conditions. Because the pathogen that causes late blight produces so many spores, and the spores can travel long distances through the air, this disease can quickly spread beyond garden walls.

If Blight Is Present

We saw the potential for blight to arrive with spring, back in April. If the growing season is warm and humid, blight is likely, and a preventive application of a copper fungicide will be necessary to protect your other plants from infection. Infection occurs only when the leaves are wet. For home gardeners the only available fungicides that are effective against blight are protectant materials, which means that they must be on the foliage *before* spores land on leaves. Organic gardeners should look for OMRI-listed fungicides that specifically list late blight as one of the fungi they control. Read and follow label instructions carefully! And be aware: copper can be toxic to plants if it builds up over time, so use judiciously and don't overapply.

If you choose not to use fungicide, again, it is crucial that you frequently check your plants especially during June Gloom weather patterns and remove and destroy infected plants to avoid spreading the disease. If possible, destroy infected plants on a dry, sunny day (not too much wind either) when dislodged spores will die quickly. If the weather is continuously wet, it is better to destroy plants sooner rather than waiting for a dry day.

SKILL SET

SKILL SET: HOME REMEDIES FOR POWDERY MILDEW

GARLIC

Blend two bulbs of fresh garlic in a quart of water with a few drops of liquid soap. Strain the liquid through cheesecloth to remove solids and then refrigerate. Dilute the concentrate 1:10 with water before spraying. The active element, allicin, will help prevent germination of powdery mildew spores. Once the spores are active, though, repeated applications will be needed to cure powdery mildew.

COMPOST TEA

Many organic growers have had great results and champion the benefits of compost tea. I know the antifungal properties of compost tea well, as I've used it for years. There are some very fine compost tea bags on the market, but you can easily make it at home by mixing 1 part of finished compost (green manure compost seems to work best) with 6 parts of water. Let it soak for about a week, then strain and dilute with water until it's the color of tea.

·JULY·

SUMMER'S HERE

It's here—your garden's time to shine! But with higher temperatures come rapid growth and higher demands on every resource: water, soil nutrients, pest and disease controls and, most importantly, you! Summer in SoCal can present very different challenges, depending on where you are: South Coast has a high dew point and the occasional fog bank and monsoonal flow; in inland valleys, it's drying winds and heat waves as well as the risk of wild fires. Watering adequately and efficiently is Job 1, especially under drought conditions. Remember that most edibles equal roses and turfgrass in their thirstiness, but they can adjust to (and will even prefer) less frequent but deeper irrigation as they mature.

TO DO THIS MONTH

PLAN

- Journal it! Look back, note present conditions, and think forward: it's time to plan your fall planting list
- Order your fall seeds this month so you can begin direct sowing next month

PREPARE AND MAINTAIN

- Include wildflowers in your gardens, hedgerows, and other habitats, to attract beneficial insects and birds
- Keep beneficial insects around by using pesticides and insecticides (even organic ones) sparingly
- Continue to monitor closely for pests and disease
- Pull weeds!
- Watch to see if your plants need additional nitrogen fertilizer: increasing temperatures will ramp up plant growth rates
- Taper off the nitrogen fertilizer and side-dress with an organic phosphorus fertilizer to promote bloom and fruit set, once fruiting plants are established and blooms appear
- Be especially water-wise, whether you have a drip irrigation system or are watering by hand

SOW AND PLANT

- Continue to succession sow quick-maturing crops for a continuing harvest and maximum yield
- Do one last planting of warm-season edibles, beans and cucumber
- Plant cool-tolerant tomatoes for a late harvest through October

HARVEST

- amaranth
- artichokes
- basil
- beans
- chives
- corn
- cucumber
- dragonfruit
- edamame
- eggplant
- fenugreek
- garlic
- okra
- oregano
- peas
- peppers
- rhubarb
- strawberries
- thyme
- tomatillos
- tomatoes
- watermelon
- zucchini

Drip Irrigation

There's no getting around it—in SoCal, we must be water-wise! We live in a semi-arid, Mediterranean environment. Our landscapes are kept green and lush because of the water that is brought down south from the eastern Sierra Nevada—certainly not from our natural rainfall. So, I love you, drip irrigation: there simply is no better way to deliver water to plants. This low-volume method is at least 90% efficient (overhead sprinklers are 65 to 75% efficient), with less water lost to evaporation, wind drift, and overspray. Drip irrigation causes less soil erosion and nutrient leaching. And, since it avoids wetting leaves as overhead sprinklers do, it does not promote disease.

California has an ancient history of drought episodes, even what experts categorize as mega-droughts, which make the droughts of the 20th and 21st century seem almost insignificant. Drought, unfortunately, is something we Californians will need to deal with, and one way to do it is to make our landscapes more water efficient and productive. Using low-volume drip irrigation is a great step in the right direction.

One of the loveliest qualities of drip irrigation is how adaptable the system is. Designing a drip layout for an edible garden is pretty straightforward, as most edibles need about the same amount of water—but it is not constant throughout an edible plant's life span. For instance, tomatoes and peppers like to be kept evenly moist in the early stages of development and blossom set, but when these plants are setting fruit they enjoy a bit less water to improve the taste of the fruit (sweeter tomatoes and hotter peppers). A drip system lends itself perfectly to this kind of customization. Simply by using an emitter that allows you to reduce the flow of water (or even to close it entirely), you can address the individual needs of a plant without impacting the rest of the plants in the bed. Genius!

Remember that sandier soil textures have little water retention as well as less capillary action (water spreading from a wet to dry area, especially on the horizontal plane) as compared to heavier soils, so emitters should be placed closer together. Soil texture should also be considered when deciding duration and intervals of watering. In lighter soils, the duration would be shorter but with more frequent intervals. Clayey soil textures have very good water retention and capillary action, meaning emitters can be placed farther apart. Heavier soil would also allow more time between watering because it drains more slowly.

Reaching the Root Zone

The objective of irrigation is to get the appropriate amount of water required by the plant to its root zone most efficiently. Obviously the depth of a plant's rooting zone will change as the plant matures, but knowing the ultimate rooting depth of the plant is important to keep in mind when adjusting irrigation. For example, when any plant is newly germinated or seedling transplanted, the root zones exist within the top few inches of soil, so irrigation needs only to wet the first few inches. Be aware that roots that shallow will dry quickly, especially in hot or windy conditions, so intervals should be more frequent but of shorter duration at this stage. However, as healthy plants grow, their root zones will deepen toward their mature depth. To encourage this, water for a longer time but at less frequent intervals. The deeper the water penetrates, the less susceptible the moisture is

CROP	MATURE ROOTING DEPTH	CROP	MATURE ROOTING DEPTH
beans	2 feet	eggplant	14 to 16 inches
beets	2 to 3 feet	lettuce	9 to 12 inches
broccoli	12 to 14 inches	onions	1½ feet
cabbage	18 to 36 inches	peas	2½ feet
carrots	18 to 24 inches	potatoes	1½ to 2 feet
cauliflower	12 to 14 inches	tomatoes	3 to 4 feet
corn	2½ feet	watermelons	2½ to 3 feet
cucumber	1½ feet	zucchini	16 to 18 inches

to the drying effects of the environment, so it remains available to the roots. The mistake many gardeners make in a mature garden is assuming the plants need water when the top of the soil looks dry. I advise my clients and students to always feel the soil, either by inserting a finger or moisture meter or even digging a small hole into the soil. This usually reveals adequate moisture at rooting zone depths.

Farmscaping

Yes, beneficial insects can be bought, but why not get them to come to the garden—and stay—for free? The strategy is called farmscaping (Robert Bugg of UC Davis coined the term), and it's used in organic farming as a whole-farm ecological approach to attract and nurture the populations of beneficial insects. It is entirely possible to integrate this technique into the home garden. Components of farmscaping include the following:

Insect host plants. Dedicate 5 to 10% of your garden space to include flowering plants that will attract and keep beneficials. The goal is to have a selection of plants that will bloom throughout the year—perennials like asters, lavender, milkweeds, penstemons, and queen anne's lace.

Hedgerows. A hedgerow is an ancient Roman technique of using a row of trees or shrubs as an agricultural border. Much like the edges of natural forests, these

EDIBLES THAT PROVIDE FOOD AND SHELTER FOR BENEFICIAL INSECTS

- basil
- celery
- cilantro
- dill
- fennel
- thyme

layered barriers provide various habitats from nesting sites for birds to windbreaks for the garden. Rodents a problem? Plant more rosemary (a hedgerow of rosemary around your garden beds is perfect), and let your peppermint or spearmint run (pull some up if it goes out of bounds).

Cover crops. Cover crops are used to reinvigorate the fertility and structure of soil in spring or fall. What's more, clover and many other cover crops bloom, and their flowers attract many pollinators and beneficials. These "green manure" crops, as they are sometimes called, include peas, clover, radish, rye, wheat, oats, and fava beans.

Water reservoirs. To complete the habitat, gardens need to include a reservoir for water of some kind. It can be as simple as a concave rock, a birdbath, or a fountain (don't use bleach or chemicals to clean them, please).

SKILL SET

SKILL SET: A SIMPLE DIY BIRDBATH

MATERIALS

three terracotta pots—large, medium, and small

large terracotta saucer

waterproof adhesive caulk

nontoxic terracotta sealer (like Mod Podge)

STEPS

1 Invert and stack the pots on top of each other, large pot on bottom.
2 Use the nontoxic sealer to paint and seal the saucer to make it retain water well.
3 Use the adhesive caulk to attach the saucer to the top pot.
4 Fill saucer with water.

You can also paint the pots and even mosaic the inside of the saucer with broken ceramic pieces.

·AUGUST·

PEAK O' THE SEASON

It's hot out here! The garden is pumping and glorious. We've enjoyed quick-maturing crops since March but now see the potential of the warm-season harvest to come. For me, the arrival of high summer is a collage of images: dangling grapes, elegant eggplants, and, yes, as it is for so many, heirloom tomatoes, their jeweled heritage on grand display. The farmscaping done last month is now doing the job, bringing in beneficial insects, birds, and pollinators—all is good. This is one of the best times to pull out the camera/phone and snap some pictures of the garden at its peak, because a good picture is worth a thousand journal words!

TO DO THIS MONTH

PLAN

- Journal with next year in mind by including your current garden photos
- Sort through your seeds and plan your fall garden planting calendar: soil amendment, direct sowing, and seedling transplants (of course, the execution of your cool-season plan will depend on weather)

PREPARE AND MAINTAIN

- Keep your garden wildlife-friendly by continuing to make room for farmscaping
- Continue to monitor closely for pests and disease—caterpillars are the bane of the garden now, so be vigilant!
- Pull weeds!
- Give your hardworking garden a "shot in the arm" with a mid-season addition of compost and earthworm castings
- Continue your water-wise ways; be sure your drip irrigation system in particular is in good working order and adjusted to current plant needs and weather

SOW AND PLANT

- Plant warm-season edibles—this is the last hoorah for beans and cucumbers, and last chance to plant transplants of Brussels sprouts so that they will be on your holiday dinner plate by December
- Continue to succession sow quick-maturing crops for a continuing harvest, but give heat-sensitive plants some afternoon shade and do not let them dry out
- Switch to heat-tolerant varieties of arugula and lettuce: South Coast should be able to grow these throughout the summer (with afternoon sun protection), but inland valleys may find the heat index to be too harsh for these sensitive greens and will need to wait until fall to plant again

HARVEST

- amaranth
- basil
- beans
- chives
- corn
- cucumber
- dragonfruit
- edamame
- eggplant
- fenugreek
- garlic
- grapes
- okra
- oregano
- peas
- peppers
- strawberries
- thyme
- tomatillos
- tomatoes
- watermelon
- zucchini

Lay Some Sugar on Me

Sugar is the secret to flavorful fruit. Fruits, like people, get better as they mature. And like people, the process of maturing has a lot to do with hormones. The hormone that triggers ripening in fruits and vegetables is ethylene. A synthetic version of this gas is what growers spray onto fruits harvested before they are ripe to stimulate ripening while en route to the market. While this synthetic ethylene gas will work to change the color of fruit, it can't develop the sugars—that is why so many supermarket fruits seem tasteless. Here's how it works. Ethylene initiates the softening of the cellular walls, making them pliable and porous, which allows the mixing of phenolic compounds (including flavonoids) that help build the color, flavor, juice development, and mouthfeel of fresh fruits.

Flavonoids are well-known antioxidants that have been shown to decrease heart disease. When fruit is left to sit on the plant too long, overripening can reduce the amount of these flavonoids, which makes harvesting at the right time even more important. Ripening is the end of the fruiting process that began with a blossom. It is extremely important for the gardener to be aware and watchful of this, the final stage of the plant's life cycle, to be sure to harvest the fruit at the right moment in

BRIX-A-BRAC, OR USING A REFRACTOMETER

Most market growers, vintners, and many chefs count this small tool among their most important. The refractometer measures the sugar content in fruit on the Brix scale (0 to 32, the higher the number, the sweeter the fruit). Testing around the last stages of ripening can exactly pinpoint the peak of flavor, and for our chef clients, flavor is everything. For an investment of around $60, you too can have the key to Flavor Town. Here's a "Brix table" of some of our favorite edibles:

VEGGIE/FRUIT	POOR	AVERAGE	GOOD	EXCELLENT
beets	6	8	10	12
cucumber	4	6	8	12
grapes	8	12	16	20
peas	4	6	10	12
peppers (bell)	4	6	8	12
strawberries	6	10	14	16
tomatoes	4	6	8	10
watermelon	8	12	14	16
zucchini	4	8	12	14

order to enjoy the "fruit" of your labor at its peak flavor and nutritional value.

You've done everything else right—watered correctly, managed soil fertility properly, and controlled pests and disease—now the rest is up to the plant and the weather.

Bring on the Heat

Fruits need the sunshine and heat of the warm-season garden to finish the ripening process successfully. Both are necessary to convert their simple sugars (glucose) into more complex sugars (fructose and sucrose). Optimum temperature range for ripening fruit on the plant is 68 to 77°F. When temperatures dip to 55°F, ripening is delayed by about 2 weeks, and there won't be any ripening at all when nighttime temperatures dip below 50°F and daytime temperatures are below 60°F for 2 weeks or more.

The South Coast is most likely to be dealing with summers of "shy" sun—think marine layer, or extended monsoonal flow coming up from Baja. At our urban farm in Venice, we've faced this every summer: although our tomatoes develop in size (albeit much more slowly than those of our inland valley brethren), their flavor can stay stubbornly sour (less than 6 on the Brix scale) if the sun doesn't shine consistently.

SKILL SET

SKILL SET: DIY HERB DRYING RACK IDEAS

Drying herbs is easier than you think! All you need is good air circulation in a dry environment so the herbs won't mold. Harvest the herbs mid-morning. Tie stems in bundles and hang the herbs upside down. Wrap with cheesecloth or a paper bag, tied around the stems. Herbs should retain their flavor for 6 to 12 months.

- Hang an expandable wooden laundry drying rack and tie your herb bundles to it.
- Lean an old stepladder against a wall or attach to ceiling, and tie your herb bundles to the rungs.
- Collect old plant or coat wall hooks of all different shapes and sizes from garage sales and flea markets. Arrange them on the wall of your pantry and hang your bundles from them.

·SEPTEMBER·

HARVEST TO TABLE
AND BEYOND

Here in SoCal our vegetable gardens are still going strong, with plants blooming and fruiting like mad. This is often the most productive month, in fact—especially during summers when the monsoonal flow lingers and delays the true heat of summer. If cool-tolerant tomatoes were planted in July, they should be taking off now. And (I know this well myself) you're probably on your third round of zucchini bread by now, with your neighbors taking cover as you approach, loaf and harvest basket in hand. Ah, the bounty! Inevitably, our thoughts turn to somehow preserving these jewels of summer. Think you can't? You *can*!

TO DO THIS MONTH

PLAN

- Look back in your journal notes from March for tips on gracefully navigating this second shoulder season (in SoCal, the transition from summer to fall happens somewhere between now and November).
- Look back in your journal notes for last fall's weather patterns and challenges; it will help you decide what plants you'll leave in the ground to produce seeds to save for next summer

- Research any plants on your cool-season planting list that are new to you
- Finalize your fall planting plan, making adjustments for current and developing weather patterns that may preclude or postpone the choices you made: who wants a bed full of bolting broccoli, cabbage, cauliflower, and lettuce?

PREPARE AND MAINTAIN

- Be ready to reassess and adapt your plans as Mother Nature figures out when she wants to let go of summer and embrace fall—there is still a chance of late heat waves in all areas even though the day length is shortening and the nighttime temperatures are beginning to cool
- Welcome wildlife: if you did a solid farmscaping plan in the summer and included some plants that will provide food (berries) and shelter (branches) for our wild birds through the fall and winter, you'll keep them in your garden throughout the year. I usually put my hummingbird and bird feeders away in summer, as I'd much rather wildlife is fed from

my farmscape plants than from a feeder, but now is the time to take them out and fill them in order to ensure a continuing food supply until your fall farmscape plants start producing.
- Continue to monitor closely for pests and disease: caterpillars remain the bane of the garden, so be vigilant!
- Pull weeds!
- Amend your tired soil with a rich compost
- Continue to monitor your drip irrigation system to make sure all is in working order, and continue to adjust the irrigation timer to compensate for weather patterns

SOW AND PLANT

- Continue to succession sow quick-maturing crops for a continuing harvest, but give heat-sensitive plants some afternoon shade and do not let them dry out. Switch (if you haven't already) to heat-tolerant varieties. South Coast should continue to be able to grow these (with afternoon sun protection), but inland valleys may find the heat index is still too harsh for these sensitive greens: arugula, Asian greens, chard, cilantro, kale, lettuce, radicchio

HARVEST

- amaranth
- arugula
- basil
- beans
- chives
- cucumber
- dragonfruit
- edamame
- eggplant
- fenugreek
- garlic
- grapes
- okra
- oregano
- peas
- peppers
- strawberries
- thyme
- tomatillos
- tomatoes
- watermelon
- zucchini

Preservation Nation

Well, as they say, everything old is new again. You had to figure it would happen. With the resurgence of interest in homegrown fruit and veggies, could a renewed interest in food preservation be far behind? Back when I was certified as a Master Gardener in LA County through UC Davis, they had discontinued their Master Food Preserver program—but now it's back, and with a bang! What brought it back? Popular demand, of course.

And it's not all about canning. Food can be preserved by salting, pickling, drying, and freezing, among others. The method you choose depends on the results you want—do you want to impart a different flavor to your product, or do you want to preserve, as much as possible, the state and flavor of the original crop? Here are just some of the ways you can get started down the road to preserving your garden's glory!

Canning

Canning (or jarring) is what we think about when we picture the classic pantry shelves of decades past. Your grandma knew that the idea of canning is simple: processing food in jars at very high temperatures for extended periods of time causes the microorganisms and enzymes that could cause spoilage to die or become inactive. The high temperatures create a vacuum seal as the food cools. This prevents the microorganism-laden air from entering the jar and contaminating the food.

There are two types of canning techniques. In raw-packing, freshly prepared (unheated) food is tightly packed into jars. These foods will float in the jars. Raw-packing is perfect for pickles and vegetables processed in a pressure canner. In hot-packing, you heat freshly prepared food to boiling, let simmer 2 to 5 minutes, and immediately fill jars loosely with the boiled food. Whichever process you use, the juice, syrup, or water to be added to the foods must be heated to boiling prior to being added to the jars.

Pickling

I'm having a long-term love affair with pickles. The wondrous ways you can alter the taste of your favorite veggies—from sour briny saltiness to the beautiful heat of spice and even the ultimate umami of sweet and sour—make me adore this type of preserving. And I'm not the only one. Take a look through your favorite farmers' market—pickles, pickles everywhere! I think making pickles is the easiest way to preserve. Pickling is perfect for beginners since the high acid content requires less processing and the raw-packing technique allows the raw vegetable to retain its delicious crispness.

Freezing

Preserving food by freezing is a safe, easy, and convenient method for fruits, vegetables, and herbs. Since edibles begin to degrade immediately after harvest, it is important to freeze your produce as soon after harvest as possible in order to preserve peak flavor and nutritional value.

Vegetables. To help retain the color and texture of your vegetables when freezing, blanch them first. Immerse your cut and cleaned veggies in boiling water for just a few minutes and then place them into a bath of ice water. This stops the cooking process and locks in color. Thoroughly dry the vegetables and pack tightly into containers or freezer bags. Just make sure to squeeze as much air out of the containers or bags as possible. Place in freezer. Your frozen vegetables will hold for 12 to 18 months at 0°F or lower.

Tomatoes. Wash tomatoes. In order to remove skins, dip whole tomatoes in boiling water for 30 seconds, then remove loosened skins and remove core. Pack into containers or freezer bags, leaving 1-inch headspace. Remove as much air as possible and freeze.

Berries. Simply wash, sort, and place in container or freezer bag. Remove as much air as possible.

Herbs. Gently wash the herbs with leaves left on the stems. Shake excess water off and place on paper towels to drain and dry. To use whole: place the cleaned herbs into a container or freezer bag removing as much air as possible; place in freezer. To use diced: cut up washed herbs to the desired size and pack into ice cube trays; freeze trays and then pop out cubes and place into freezer bags removing as much air as possible.

Drying

Drying is the oldest method of preserving food. This was an integral part of food preservation for ancient peoples, who did it without any fancy tools or equipment—which tells you drying will be an easy and low-tech process at home. Added bonus: because the moisture content is so low, dried foods keep very well. Key components are low humidity, low constant heat (120 to 150°F), and good air circulation. Of course, you can purchase a wonderful dehydrator, but you can certainly get the job done simply by using the sun, the air, or the oven.

SKILL SET

SKILL SET: GOING REALLY OLD SCHOOL, OR THE LOW-DOWN ON LOW-TECH DRYING

OVEN DRYING

No, it's not as efficient as a dehydrator (takes 2 to 3 times longer than a dehydrator), but almost all of us have an oven in our kitchens, so why not? The other time suck is due to the fact that air circulation is poor in an oven (unless you have a convection oven). It is probably a good idea to check the accuracy of your oven temperature by placing an oven thermometer inside the oven and setting the temperature to 140°F. Wait 15 to 20 minutes and check the thermometer. If you don't have a convection setting, you can leave the oven door slightly open, 2 to 4 inches, and place a fan near the outside of the oven door to help with air circulation. Shifting the trays around on the racks every now and then will help counteract the effects of cool or hot spots in the oven.

SUN DRYING

Sun drying requires constant exposure to direct sunlight during the day and a relative humidity of less than 20%. This may not be possible during most times of the year in the South Coast. High humidity will mold food before it dries. Sun-dried vegetables take 3 to 4 days to fully dry.

AIR DRYING

Air drying takes place indoors in a well-ventilated attic, room, or screened porch. Herbs, hot peppers, and mushrooms are the most common air-dried edibles. Blanch vegetables prior to air drying. Vegetables can be air dried in 4 to 12 hours, but this varies depending on the type of vegetable. When completely dry, vegetables should be hard and brittle.

·OCTOBER·

THE SLOW SLIDE

It has been a rewarding summer season—not just the harvest, which is ongoing, but all the learning, too. Remember, you will always learn more from your failures than from your successes. It might take you a few seasons on this learning curve to feel more confident, but know that as a gardener, you're never finished learning, which is why I love it. Season after season, you can look forward to and build upon small but important moments of success: improving tired soil, starting your own seeds, gathering in your first harvest, saving seeds, becoming healthier. Big or small, they are all successes. Now . . . into the cool season we go!

TO DO THIS MONTH

PLAN

- Add new sections to your garden journal for the new season
- Look back in your journal notes from last fall and decide what plants you'll leave in the ground to produce seeds to save for next summer
- Research any plants on your cool-season planting list that are new to you
- Firm up your fall planting plan!
- Be ready to reassess and adapt your plan, making adjustments for current and developing weather patterns, slowing switching from plants that fruit to plants that root

PREPARE AND MAINTAIN

- Be prepared, as September's shoulder season continues into October, for shorter but warm days and cooling nights; there is still a chance of late heat waves in all areas
- Continue to keep a watchful eye out for pests and disease
- Clean up your mess! Time to remove debris and tired old plants from the long summer
- Add fresh compost, if you haven't yet done so this fall
- Continue to monitor your drip irrigation system and make adjustments to irrigation timer to compensate for weather patterns

SOW AND PLANT

- Continue to succession sow quick-maturing crops for a continuing harvest and high yield, but give heat-sensitive plants some afternoon shade and do not let them dry out during any fall heat waves (you will find that arugula and Asian greens will grow even better with the nights cooling a bit now)

TO DO THIS MONTH CONTINUED

HARVEST

- amaranth
- arugula
- Asian greens
- basil
- beans
- dragonfruit
- eggplant

- fenugreek
- garlic
- grapes
- okra
- oregano
- peas
- peppers

- strawberries
- thyme
- tomatillos
- tomatoes
- watermelon
- zucchini

Cornucopia

October, a lovely dance between light and dark, warm and cool, has traditionally been the month our farming ancestors celebrated the bounty of the harvest. It is the month when we continue the slow slide into the cool season, experiencing gradually shortening days and cooling nights. This time of year, like the spring equinox, is a very special moment in our natural year, marking the ending of one cycle and the beginning of another, the end of the light half of the year and the beginning of the dark half, in this hemisphere.

It is also the month that opens the legendary Santa Ana wind season in SoCal. These wind episodes can happen any time between now and March, so stay tuned to weather forecasts. If you've newly planted your tender

SOLSTICE AND EQUINOX

Ever get confused about the difference?

Solstice. Winter (21 December) and spring (21 June) solstice is when the sun is at its furthest point from the equator.

Equinox. Fall (22 September) and spring (20 March) equinox is when the sun is closest to the equator, resulting in equal day and night lengths.

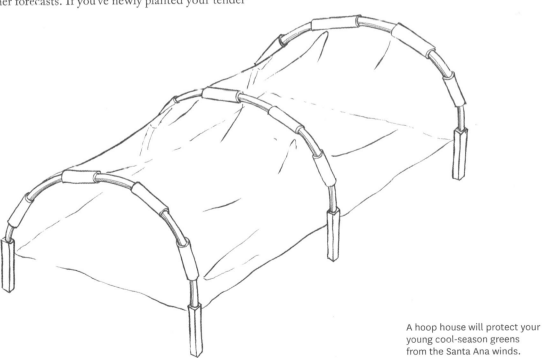

A hoop house will protect your young cool-season greens from the Santa Ana winds.

cool-season greens, be ready to protect them in their young stage from these hot, dry winds. You can do this a few different ways:

- Use or build hoop houses (see March's Skill Set) or windbreaks
- Remember that Santa Anas come out of the northeast and blow offshore, so plant your tender greens on the southwest side of a taller, dense plant, a fence, hedgerow, or structure. This will protect them from the direct, desiccating damage of these winds.
- Plant a windbreak. This is also helpful if you've had to site your garden on a particularly windy site anyway. Observe the prevailing wind direction and plan your row of trees or tall shrubs so that the windbreak will do the job of buffering these winds.

Clean Your Room

After a long, very busy summer battling pest and disease pressures and struggling to keep an overstressed soil fertile, watered, and in balance, we are looking forward to cooling temperatures, short days, and a whole different plant scape. I adore the fall, but like spring, it can give us conflicting messages. Yes, the days are shortening and nights are cooling, but we can still experience summer-like heat waves, so we balance with one foot in summer and one foot in fall. The bright side of that scenario is that you can get one last flush of late-season tomatoes and the other lingering jewels of summer this month. This indecisiveness on Mother Nature's part will also give you an opportunity to get end-of-season chores done.

Tidying up between summer and fall is very important. Although I normally like to leave healthy debris on the soil surface as an added organic bonus, when there was disease in the garden we cannot be so passive. Good hygiene is one of the ways we can control blight and other diseases from reinfecting our garden in the next warm season, so pick up, bag up, and put the trash out. Yes, in the trash, not the compost. You do not want to contaminate the city's mulch/compost program.

Your Soil's Hungry— Feed It!

By this time of year, your soil is tired and depleted. Make sure you've amended with rich compost or leaf mold, adding a nice 2- to 3-inch layer before you plant out your cool-season garden. If you have an abundance of healthy leaf debris building up in your yard, by all means, use it as mulch. If it's been a particularly brutal summer season, there is another option to give your soil a little "shot in the arm"—cover cropping. Cover cropping isn't only for large farms. It is an easy process to apply to home gardens as well. This process of growing and then tilling in "green manure" has been used for centuries. A cover crop can be planted in the very early spring as well as fall. It is important to time it so that killing frosts are avoided. Cover crops help build soil structure and fix nitrogen after they're tilled under and left to decompose for about 3 weeks before planting your garden.

SKILL SET

....

SKILL SET: COVER CROPPING

....

STEPS

1 Planting. This really is as easy as broadcasting seed into a clean bed that you've worked lightly with a garden rake. Pull soil over the seed gently with the rake.

2 Taking care. This is a low-maintenance process. If you plant a larger crop, mowing once or twice helps keeps them manageable and, in some cases, stimulates root growth. Cover crops typically have low-water needs but be sure to keep them evenly moist, especially if there is little natural rainfall.

3 Tilling in. To avoid allowing your cover crop to reseed, be sure to take it down before it sets seeds. Pull, chop, mow, and then till in the crop. Or, if you have chickens, you can let them loose in the cover crop, and they will take it down for you.

·NOVEMBER·

THE COOL SEASON

Ahh, the heat waves are (mostly) done, and the garden transition to the cool season is complete. November in SoCal can offer a wide range of weather conditions, from sunny, even hot days to wind and rainstorms, which can swiftly change things in the garden. As we have put our cool-season babies in the ground recently, we gardeners must be prepared to protect, protect, protect, from a potential downpour, wind, and chill. Production shifts to reproduction, with flowers becoming interesting seed pods and leaves falling to reveal the beautiful bones of the garden—a fitting artful backdrop to your cool-season edibles. Where others might see only decay and debris, you see nature's art box.

TO DO THIS MONTH

PLAN

- Look back in your journal notes for the last cool season's likes and dislikes, successes and failures. When did soil cool down to 40 to 45°F?
- Be sure your fall garden plan includes all the herbs, greens, and roots that you'll need for your table from Thanksgiving on to the end of the holiday season
- Plan ahead to make gifts of herb vinegars (blends like basil/garlic, basil/chive, garlic/chive): they take 4 to 6 weeks

PREPARE AND MAINTAIN

- Watch for developing Santa Ana wind events
- Be prepared for early frost warnings in the inland valleys, ready to protect crops with hoop houses, cold frames, and straw mulches
- Finish garden clean up
- Adjust your irrigation system to the changing weather and the new cool-season garden layout; reprogram your timer as weather patterns (rain, cooling nights, high dew points) shift

SOW AND PLANT

- Continue to succession sow quick-maturing crops for a continuing harvest and high yield, but give tender young plants some protection during frost, wind, and rain events (arugula, Asian greens, and lettuce will grow even better with the cool nights)

HARVEST

- amaranth
- arugula
- Asian greens
- broccoli
- dragonfruit
- fenugreek
- French tarragon
- garlic
- lettuce
- oregano
- peas
- strawberries
- thyme
- tomatillos
- watermelon

Gather in the Garden

With the end of the season that focused us outward, comes the season that will focus us inward toward home and hearth and the celebrations to come—and you are ready! In the coastal zones we are happy to see the occasional fog bank return with our cooling nights and rejoice in the mild days of bright, albeit less potent sunshine. In the inland valleys, nights are cooling fast, with the occasional chance of a light frost starting later in the month through February. Sunny days in SoCal are still more likely now than not, but the rainy season, when it does rain, spans November through March. Your summer garden jewels have been frozen, pickled, jarred, or otherwise preserved for use on the holiday table or as gifts. The cool-season plants are neatly tucked into their garden beds, and the garden is in its quiet growing mode with protection from any threatening weather shift at the ready.

This month marks the beginning of the holiday season for most, bringing with it a gradual ratcheting up of stress and pressures as plans and commitments are made. We're probably finding less time for the very thing that is our biggest stress reliever—our garden! One way to get family and friends active and out there with us in the garden is to have a holiday garden hunt. Get the kids (young and old) together Thanksgiving Day and send them out into your garden or a nearby park or wooded space to search for natural materials that could be made into holiday décor—interesting branches, leaves, pine cones, rose hips, seed pods, fruits, berries, or anything else that would make a beautiful wreath, centerpiece, or candle décor. Can you think of a better way to get your kids and their friends to disconnect, unplug, and power down—get back to the simpler, more human way to celebrate the holidays, get them to actually go outside? Remind them—they're in Southern California. It's a playground, 365 days a year!

NUTRITIONAL POWERHOUSES OF THE COOL-SEASON GARDEN: GREENS

arugula	Contains vitamins A, C, and K, calcium, magnesium, riboflavin, copper, iron, zinc, folate, and potassium as well as being high in antioxidants. Helps control blood pressure and osteoporosis.
beet greens	High in potassium and iron. Fights free radicals, cancer, and heart disease. May help fight Alzheimer's disease.
kale	Most nutrient-dense of leafy greens, high in calcium and vitamin K. Has anti-cancer benefits. Promotes healthy bones and vision (retinal function). Helps to regulate blood sugar and prevents arthritis.
turnip greens	High in antioxidants, potassium, calcium, and iron. Boosts immune system.

Your garden will welcome the help of many extra pairs of hands doing the last bit of clean up and putting its fallen canopy and fruit to good use. And a holiday garden hunt will help focus your family, friends, and neighbors on activities that, besides bringing you all together, provide the calming and decompressing effects of simply being out in nature—something we do too little of these days.

THE HOLIDAY HERB GARDEN

chives	A wonderful partner in salads, potato dishes (mashed or roasted), poultry, latke-topping sauces
dill	Peas, fish, latke-topping sauces
French tarragon	Poultry, potatoes, mushrooms, salad dressing, latke-topping sauces, eggs
thyme	Poultry, pork, tomato, veggies, bread

SKILL SET

SKILL SET: HOLIDAY WREATH

MATERIALS

garden beauty gathered on your holiday garden hunt (pine cones, rose hips, seed pods, berries), including green bendable boughs (flat leaf cedar, eucalyptus, bottlebrush) and woody material (willow branches, grape vines, sprigs of boxwood, pittosporum, ficus, olive)

florist wire, pruners, wire snips

STEPS

1 If the plant material is very bendable (flat leaf cedar), just wire overlapping sections together in one 6- to 8-foot strand, and then coil it into a circle and wire the layers together.

2 If the greens don't bend easily, cut them into 8-inch lengths and wire the overlapping ends together until you get the size and shape you want.

3 Add decorative elements—moss, pine cones, nuts, berries, herb bundles, rose hips, sprigs of boxwood and ferns—onto the wreath by twisting wire around the element and through the wreath, securing it tightly by twisting the wire ends.

4 Use wire to form a hook for the wreath.

·DECEMBER·

OUR GARDEN'S GIFTS

We continue to be blessed by what is a very mild winter season compared to what most other North American gardeners suffer through at this time of year. Aside from the occasional hard frost in the inland valleys or the once-in-a-decade severe wet El Niño winter, in most years there just aren't that many harsh weather episodes to deal with. That means that, though growing at a slower rate than in the warm season, our winter gardens still deliver a beautiful look and amazingly bountiful produce. And even in winter, if we look carefully, we can still find plenty of wildlife in our gardens enjoying the winter abundance we've nurtured. The phrase "dead of winter" just doesn't apply in SoCal.

TO DO THIS MONTH

PLAN

- Look back in your journal notes for the last cool season's weather patterns and challenges
- Make notes about the current weather patterns and what severe events are predicted (heavy rain, hard frosts, wind)

PREPARE AND MAINTAIN

- Be prepared for frost in the inland valleys and ready to protect crops with hoop houses covered with fleece, cold frames, and straw mulches
- Adjust irrigation to the changing weather; remember to turn off your system when rain comes

SOW AND PLANT

- Continue to succession sow quick-maturing crops for a continuing harvest and higher yield, but give tender young plants some protection during frost, wind, and rain events (arugula, kale, lettuce and radicchio are now thriving in the cooler temperatures)

HARVEST

- amaranth
- arugula
- asparagus
- Brussels sprouts
- cabbage
- carrots
- cauliflower
- chives
- corn
- dragonfruit
- fennel
- fenugreek
- French tarragon
- garlic
- kale
- leeks
- lettuce
- oregano
- parsnips
- peas
- radicchio
- thyme
- turnips

CYA (Cover Your Agriculture)

By now, especially in the inland valleys, you've trained yourselves to listen to your local meteorologist or downloaded that weather app on your devices and check it often. The weather patterns are changing, and we have to look for every forecasted shift if we are to protect our garden and landscape. This can mean everything from cutting back your shrubs and brush during fire season if you live in a high-risk zone to being ready to put hoop houses over your vegetable garden. The point is to be ready. Here are some frost-centric tips:

- Water soil thoroughly. I know it is counter-intuitive, but the reality is that wet soil holds heat better than dry soil. Wet soil also protects roots and keeps the air near the top of soil warmer.
- Know your garden's microclimates. You can protect container plants by clustering them close together in the warmest area of your yard, usually a protected spot on the leeward side of a structure.
- Use cold frames or hoop houses. Agricultural fleece in varying thicknesses is available for purchase.
- If you don't have time to purchase or build your cold frame or hoop house, you can also use bed sheets, drop cloths, blankets, and plastic sheets to cover your plants. Make sure that you use stakes of some kind to keep the material from coming into contact with foliage.
- For a short cold snap, low plants can be covered with mulch like straw or leaf mold.
- Be prompt about removing all coverings as soon as the temperature rises the next day (especially important if you're using plastic).

'Tis the Season

And . . . we're in the thick of it: the holiday season. While the garden quiets down, our lives do not—what with work, family, and social commitments and all the planning and gifting to get done. Well, your garden can be your helping hand, providing produce for your holiday menu and gifts for those on your "nice" list. With any luck, you tried August's Skill Set, and now have a bounty of dried herbs that you can make into lovely hostess gifts like aromatherapy sachets or culinary herb bundles. But those are just a couple of possibilities. The garden's gift-giving potential is great. Here are some other ideas:

- Culinary herb kitchen table wreath. Wire together a wreath of flat leaf cedar and nestle into it an assortment of dried herbs (from your garden) and spices, wrapped in cheesecloth bundles and tied with red ribbon, for seasoning soups, poultry, omelets, bread, meats, spiced cider, etc. Tie labels to bundles, describing contents and use.
- Herb jellies. Try thyme jelly (for beef or fish) or basil jelly (on hot rolls).
- Compound butters. A wonderful butter blended with your garden herbs, whether fresh or dried, make a perfect gift for the cook on your list.

SKILL SET

SKILL SET: COMPOUND BUTTER LOG

Nothing is easier or more appreciated by a home cook than handmade gifts using herbs and veggies you've grown yourself. Dress it all up in beautiful wrapping, and you'll be on *their* "nice" list forever! Compound butters could not be an easier culinary gift. The two main ingredients—butter and the chopped herbs—are basically used in the same proportions, but the nice thing is you can add or subtract, adjusting to taste, to make the recipe your very own. Here are two flavor combos, for a start: tarragon and two finely diced shallots, with salt and white pepper to taste; thyme and the zest of one lemon, with black pepper. Have fun coming up with your own!

INGREDIENTS

1 lb. unsalted butter (room temperature)

¼ cup chopped combined herbs (take your time and do a fine dice)

parchment paper

straight edge

WRAPPING

1 Portion out the butter (½ cup makes a good gift size for each flavor—gift one or an assortment of flavors) and place into the center of a piece of parchment paper, then fold the paper from one end to the other.

2 Tuck the parchment under slightly, leaving a bit untucked.

3 With one hand holding the bottom large portion of parchment paper, gently push the butter against folded end, so that you begin compressing it into the form of a log.

4 To form the final log shape, use something that has a straight edge to compress it further (e.g., an inverted baking sheet, a pastry scraper/cutter). Working away from you with one hand holding the bottom portion of parchment paper, slide the straight edge along the open bottom piece of parchment, pressing the butter into the folded end to form a tighter, longer log. Keep doing that until you have formed a nice long log that almost fills the sheet of parchment paper.

5 Twist the ends of the parchment and refrigerate (keeps about 2 weeks) or freeze (keeps about 3 months).

You can also double-wrap the parchment-wrapped butter logs in nice butcher paper, open-weave home décor–grade burlap, muslin, or cheesecloth, and tie the ends with kitchen twine or raffia. Pretty handmade tags with the flavors of each log on them would be a nice finishing touch.

EDIBLES
A TO Z

PLANTING AND HARVESTING CHART

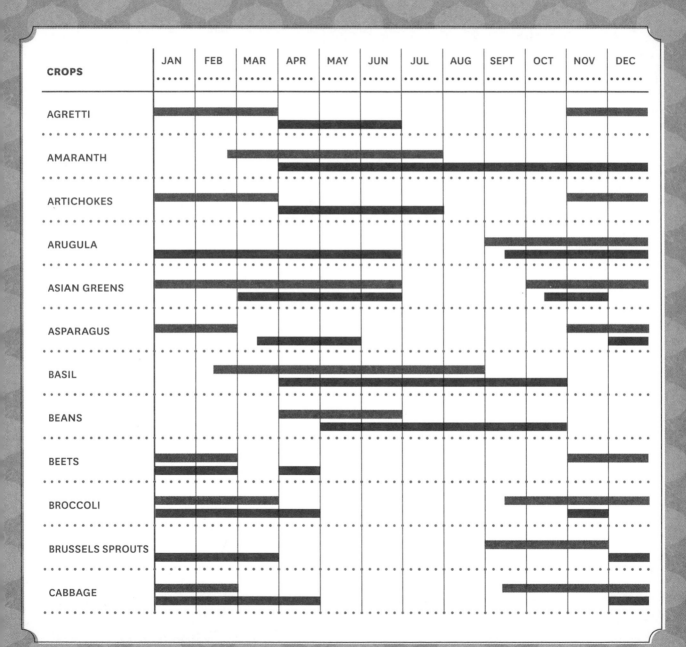

Planting
Harvesting

This chart shows the planting and harvesting ranges for edibles grown outdoors without protection in our unique SoCal climate. Dates are approximate. Exact planting dates will vary depending on your garden's microclimates and the vagaries of the weather.

CROPS	JAN	FEB	MAR	APR	MAY	JUN	JUL	AUG	SEPT	OCT	NOV	DEC
AGRETTI	███	███	██	██	██	██					█	█
AMARANTH		██	██	██	██	██	██	█				██
ARTICHOKES	██	██	██	██	██	██	██				█	█
ARUGULA	██	██	██	██	██	██	██	██	█	██	██	██
ASIAN GREENS	██	██	██	██	██	██			█	██	██	
ASPARAGUS	█	██	██	██							██	██
BASIL		█	██	██	██	██	██	██	██			
BEANS				██	██	██	██	██	██	█		
BEETS	██	██	█	██							█	██
BROCCOLI	██	██	██						█	██	██	
BRUSSELS SPROUTS	█								█	██	██	
CABBAGE	██	█							█	██		██

Planting and harvest calendar (● = shaded bar present)

CROPS	JAN	FEB	MAR	APR	MAY	JUN	JUL	AUG	SEPT	OCT	NOV	DEC
CARROTS	●	●	●							●	●	
	●	●	●	●	●							●
CAULIFLOWER	●										●	●
	●	●	●									●
CELERY	●										●	●
		●	●	●	●							
CHARD										●	●	●
		●	●	●	●	●						
CHIVES	●	●	●	●	●					●	●	●
	●	●	●	●	●	●	●	●				●
CILANTRO	●	●	●	●							●	
	●	●	●	●	●							
CORN				●	●	●	●					●
					●	●	●					●
CUCUMBER				●	●	●	●	●	●			
					●	●	●	●	●			
DILL	●	●	●								●	
	●	●	●	●								
DRAGONFRUIT			●	●	●	●						●
							●	●	●	●		
EDAMAME				●	●	●	●					
					●	●	●	●				
EGGPLANT				●	●	●	●					
					●	●	●	●	●			
FAVA BEANS	●	●								●	●	●
			●	●	●	●						
FENNEL	●	●								●	●	●
			●	●								●
FENUGREEK		●	●									
			●	●	●	●	●	●	●	●	●	●

CROPS	JAN	FEB	MAR	APR	MAY	JUN	JUL	AUG	SEPT	OCT	NOV	DEC
FRENCH TARRAGON	●	●	●	●	●	●					●	●
GARLIC			●	●	●	●	●	●	●	●	●	●
GRAPES			●	●	●	●		●	●			
KALE	●	●	●	●	●	●				●	●	●
LEEKS	●	●	●	●	●					●	●	●
LETTUCE	●	●	●	●	●	●				●	●	●
OKRA			●	●	●	●	●	●	●			
ONIONS			●	●	●					●		
OREGANO		●	●	●	●	●	●	●	●	●	●	●
PARSNIP	●	●	●								●	●
PEAS	●	●	●	●	●	●	●	●	●	●	●	●
PEPPERS				●	●	●	●	●	●	●		
POTATOES	●	●	●	●	●						●	
RADICCHIO	●	●	●	●	●						●	●
RHUBARB			●	●	●	●	●					

CROPS	JAN	FEB	MAR	APR	MAY	JUN	JUL	AUG	SEPT	OCT	NOV	DEC
STRAWBERRIES	▓	▓	▓	▓	▓							
		▓	▓	▓	▓	▓	▓	▓	▓	▓	▓	
THYME	▓	▓	▓	▓	▓	▓						
		▓	▓	▓	▓	▓	▓	▓	▓	▓	▓	▓
TOMATILLOS			▓	▓	▓	▓						
					▓	▓	▓	▓	▓	▓	▓	
TOMATOES			▓	▓	▓	▓	▓					
					▓	▓	▓	▓	▓	▓		
TURNIPS	▓	▓								▓	▓	▓
	▓		▓	▓								▓
WATERMELON		▓	▓	▓	▓	▓						
				▓	▓	▓	▓	▓	▓	▓		
ZUCCHINI			▓	▓	▓	▓						
				▓	▓	▓	▓	▓	▓	▓		

Agretti

This wild succulent native to the Mediterranean basin flourishes on many of the world's beaches. Its aliases are many (saltwort, Russian thistle, barilla plant), but agretti (its Italian name) is how most chefs know it. Young plants are used as a culinary herb; they actually taste a bit sea-salty and like spinach sprinkled with lemon. They can also be boiled, eaten raw, or used as an ingredient to add to a frittata or quiche. Imagine this fresh, slighty briny taste as a steamed bed under a beautifully prepared fish.

GROWING Agretti requires full sun and a cool climate and prefers loose, light soil, rich in organic matter and with a near neutral pH. As a seaside plant, it tolerates wind well and doesn't mind salt spray. Agretti does not require a lot of water and in fact will tolerate some dry conditions.

Agretti is not available commercially and so needs to be started from seeds sown directly in the ground. This is a bit easier if done between the end of winter and the beginning of spring. Prepare the soil well before planting by adding additional organic matter. Broadcasting the seed works, or you can sow in rows about 6 inches apart. Be prepared to wait. The seeds can take a while to germinate. Because agretti's preferred soil texture is light, even sandy, renewal of organic nitrogen is necessary to keep the plant productive.

HARVESTING Harvest agretti when plants are about 5½ inches tall. The stems will go woody and branch (becoming inedible) if they are left on the plant too long. To harvest them, take a handful and cut them off about 2 inches above the ground. New shoots will develop from crown. Agretti doesn't hold for very long in the fridge—only a few days— so it is best to harvest just before you are going to use it. The usable product is the green leaves, with their bright, slightly tangy taste. Clean leaves thoroughly: they are usually full of the sandy loam the plant was grown in.

VARIETIES Look for seeds labeled **Barba di Frate**, **Salsola Soda**, and **Roscano**.

Amaranth

This ancient grain is not yet a common edible in our SoCal gardens, but it's definitely on the "what's next" list. It is what we production growers call a "root to tip" plant, used as a grain, edible flower, microgreen, colorful ornamental, leafy green, and forage crop. And it's gluten-free. This slow-growing multi-talented plant will ultimately reach a height of 2 to 8 feet.

GROWING Amaranth responds well to full sun and warm temperatures but can tolerate some afternoon shade in hot regions of the inland valleys. Growing from seed is virtually the only option as amaranth is not popular enough to be available routinely at commercial nurseries. Plant seeds no more than ½ inch deep, in fertile, well-draining, loamy soil. Soil temperature should be at least 65°F. Seeds are small and can be difficult to germinate. Keep the seedbed evenly moist as germination rate can drop significantly if bed is allowed to dry out. Once established, plants are drought tolerant. If you've recently amended your soil, further addition of fertilizer shouldn't be necessary at planting time. You can target fertilizing depending on what part of the plant you are going to use: side-dress with blood meal (nitrogen) before flowering for a more vigorous, leafy canopy; side-dress with bone meal (phosphorus) at flowering to promote flowers.

Amaranth can tolerate considerable pressure from pests without impacting production, and as a crop, it is practically disease-free. Fungal diseases can cause seedling failures, but good cultural practices and garden hygiene can manage these occurrences.

HARVESTING In order for the grain to dry properly, a hard frost has to happen, followed by a week of dry weather. This limits grain harvest to the inland valleys with the highest chance of frost. Harvesting for the leaves or flowers can happen at any time. Grain handling and storage plans should be developed before harvest begins. If you're harvesting a small amount, grain can be dried by blowing warm air across the amaranth. The optimum way to store the grain after cleaning and drying is in wooden storage bins or in heavy duty (4- or 5-ply) paper bags.

VARIETIES **Aurelia's Verde Amaranth** (from Guatemala) and **Congo Amaranth** (from the Republic of Congo) are both green flowerers; the young leaves of the latter are amazing cooked like spinach. **Love-Lies-Bleeding** is a red-flowering old heirloom (pre-1700); leaves are delicious as cooked greens. **Poinsettia Mix Amaranth** really lights up an edible landscape with its tricolor flowers: green with creamy top leaves, rose red to chocolate brown, and bright red-orange.

Artichokes

The artichoke, a member of the milk thistle family, is thought to be native to Arabia, the Mediterranean, Iran, and Turkey. Artichokes are high in antioxidants, and in some cultures and herbal medicine practices, their leaves are used to treat liver and gallbladder problems, diabetes, high cholesterol, and hypertension, among other maladies.

GROWING Artichokes do best in frost-free coastal areas with cool foggy summers. I have successfully grown Green Globe and Imperial Star artichokes both on the coast in sandy soil and in the heavy clay (and hotter summers) of the inland valleys. Optimum temperatures are 75°F days and 55°F nights. Do not expose them to temperatures below 25°F in the winter. Artichokes are deep-rooted plants adapted to a wide range of soil types, but they perform best in well-drained, deep soil high in organic matter with a pH between 6.5 and 8.0. The artichoke is a perennial, so prepare the soil well before planting. Mix manure,

compost, or other organic matter into the first foot of soil in about equal amounts. Artichokes require frequent irrigation (water stress results in loose buds) and additional nitrogen fertilization during the growing season. Feed them in the fall with a high-nitrogen fertilizer. I use blood meal and then bone meal 6 to 8 weeks after harvest to help promote development of late buds.

These plants need leg and arm room! Width required depends on variety, but leaving about 3 feet between plants in a home garden or landscape is usually fine. I use the shade this plant eventually casts as shelter for smaller, more heat-sensitive plants that I plant around it. Aphids are a common pest. A hard stream of water can be used to remove aphids from plants. Spraying with organic insecticidal soap is also effective.

HARVESTING Harvest begins with the maturing of the first buds in fall and continues through the following spring. Peak production occurs in spring. Cut artichokes about 1 to 1½ inches below the bud base. Artichokes may be stored for 1 to 2 weeks at 32°F and freeze well.

VARIETIES My favorites, **Green Globe** and **Green Globe Improved**, are standard commercial varieties grown in coastal and other milder climates. **Imperial Star** does not need as much vernalization (exposure of plants to low temperatures in order to stimulate flowering) as these; it is thornless and primarily green, with some purple tinting. Another new variety, **Emerald**, performs in both coastal and inland valley conditions. **Purple Sicilian**, which is a deep purple, is excellent eaten raw when plants are very young.

Arugula

This delicious Mediterranean herb has been culti-vated since Roman times. A nutrient-dense green, arugula (aka rocket) has a wonderful flavor profile ranging from nutty to very peppery. There are two general classes. Salad types typically have wide, meaty leaves, rapid growth rates, and white flowers. Wild types have more narrow serrated leaves, slower growth rates, yellow flowers, and usually a sharper, spicier taste.

GROWING Arugula prefers rich, loose, well-draining soil with a neutral pH and the cooler temperatures of early spring and fall. It will grow into the hotter months on the coast with a bit of afternoon shade. Heat prompts leggy growth and flowering, which can cause the leaves to become bitter and tough. Keep arugula evenly moist.

Direct sow or transplant seedlings from a nursery. Leave about 8 to 12 inches between the salad types and 4 to 6 inches between the wild types. If you intend to harvest frequently, you can space the plants a bit closer together. Plant the seeds in shallow rows spaced 3 to 4 inches apart. Cover with ½ inch of soil, and water well. If your soil has been recently amended with compost, you won't need to be concerned about adding fertilizer immediately. Just be watchful. If you see the leaves are yellowing, or the plant doesn't seem to be thriving, go ahead and give it a foliar feed of compost tea or fish emulsion. Watch out for flea beetles and caterpillars.

HARVESTING Pick the outer leaves: the plant regenerates faster, and future harvests are guaranteed for weeks to come. Younger, smaller leaves tend to taste more mild than older, larger leaves. Store as you would other leafy greens.

VARIETIES **Astro** is a heat-tolerant variety. **Sylvetta**, a wild type, is slower growing and grows lower than its cul-tivated cousins. Leaves are deeply serrated. This type is popular among chefs. **Surrey** is similar in appearance to Sylvetta but grows a bit faster. Flavor is closer to that of the salad types. **Olive-Leaved Sylvetta** is another wild type, strongly flavored and slow growing. **Dragon's Tongue** Is a unique variety with a spicy flavor that is sought after by chefs. It has a beautiful red vein running the length of each narrow, serrated leaf. **Wasabi** is a new variety with wasabi-like heat, used mostly in Japanese dishes. Leaves are broad and spoon-shaped. Prefers cool temperatures, so plant in the cool fall or very early spring.

Asian Greens

This group of ancient greens was for years the step-child of the greens world—one foot in the mustard family, one foot in the lettuce crowd. Now they're the new darling of the professional and home kitchen alike. Usable at all sizes, Asian greens are wonderful, from microgreens to stir fries to braises.

GROWING Asian greens typically favor cool temperatures (55 to 75°F) and sunny locations, although in coastal areas they can be grown year-round with some afternoon sun protection. Never fear, inland valley gardeners: a touch of frost actually sweetens mature plants. Grow these greens in evenly moist, well-draining soil rich in organic matter, with a pH of 6.0 to 6.5.

Sow seeds about 2 inches apart and ¼ inch deep. Gently water in well. Seeds are quick to germinate. After they emerge, gradually thin them (as an intensive planter and because I tend to use Asian greens on the small side, I tend not to thin). If your soil is well amended with compost before planting, additional fertilizing might not be needed until harvesting begins. Because these are leafy greens, they should need only occasional supplemental fertilizing with a nitrogen fertilizer if your soil is healthy and fertile. You can either side-dress with blood meal or spray with liquid fish emulsion.

Common pests include slugs and snails, aphids, cabbageworms, and stink bugs. Use an organic desiccant for slugs and snails and an organic insecticidal soap for the aphids and other soft-bodied insects.

HARVESTING Timing will depend on what you're using the harvest for. Microgreens: as soon as the first true leaves appear. Baby greens: cut leaves at 3 inches long to use raw in salads. Mid-size: 4- to 6-inch leaves to use in stir fries. Full size: braises, soups. As leafy types mature, harvest individual leaves or cut away fistfuls of greens, leaving the plant's central crown intact. New leaves will quickly replace the harvested ones. Whole heads of Asian cabbages can be refrigerated for up to a month. Any Asian greens can be blanched and frozen.

VARIETIES **Tatsoi** (aka **Pak Choi**) is easy to grow, cold tolerant, and has a delicious mild mustard flavor. **Chinese Cabbage** (aka **Yukina Savoy)** looks like a larger, wrinkled (or savoyed) cousin of Tatsoi; easy to grow and both heat and cold tolerant; mild flavor when young. Chrysanthemum greens (aka **Shungiku)** have delicate serrated leaves with a lacy look I love. Harvest side shoot greens, which have mild flavor and slight aroma, and use in salads or cook like spinach. Flowers are beautiful and edible. Mustard greens include **Red Mizuna**, **Green Mizuna**, **Ruby Streak**, **Lime Streak**, **Golden Frill**, **Scarlet Frill**, **Crimson Red**, and **Giant Curled**.

Asparagus

This perennial may be in your garden longer than you will, as it lives 15 to 20 years. Choose your site carefully and put them in a section of the garden that you won't need to overly disturb. No crop rotation for this edible! A delicacy since Roman times, it's the vegetable many of us look forward to the most in spring.

GROWING Fern growth is best at 65 to 85°F. Spears start growth when temperatures reach above 50°F. The plant's growth slows below 55°F. High temperatures can cause feathering or premature opening of the spear tips. Start with deep, fertile, well-draining soil that is rich in organic matter. Loamy soil is the perfect texture, and soil should have a fine tilth at planting time. Asparagus does not perform well in acid soils; optimum soil pH is 6.0 to 6.7. Water requirements increase while the ferns are growing in spring, but be careful to avoid waterlogged roots. Drip irrigation is best. Established plants can be drought tolerant.

Order crowns (roots) that are at least a year old from a trusted seed house. Plant the crowns from January through April. Dig furrows about 12 inches deep. Form a mound on the bottom of the trench and spread the crown's roots around the mound. Gradually mound the soil over the plants as they grow until the soil is equal to the surrounding soil level. Spacing between crowns should be about 6 to 12 inches. In the fall, cut the ferns down to ground level after they turn fully brown. Broadcast an all-purpose fertilizer on the bed in spring just before the spears start to grow. A second fertilizing should be done at the end of the cutting season.

Thankfully, asparagus is not usually bothered by pests, but rust and other fungal diseases can be a problem. Good garden hygiene, using resistant plant stock, and avoiding overharvesting and overhead irrigation can help control these diseases.

HARVESTING It takes 3 years to bring your asparagus into full production. Don't harvest asparagus the first growing season after you plant the crowns. In the second year, you can cut your spears at ground level for a 2-week period; overharvesting at this point can weaken plants and reduce future harvests. In the third year you can harvest the spears for an 8- to 12-week period each spring.

VARIETIES **Jersey Knight**, a mostly male variety (male crowns are more productive than female), yields the highest quality spears of all the Jersey types, with 7- to 9-inch green spears; cold and heat tolerant; highly resistant to rust, rots, and other fungal diseases. **Mary's Granddaughter UC-72**, developed at UC Davis, has more heat and drought tolerance than others; yields heavy dark green spears with fairly compact heads; open-pollinated. **Farmer's Favorite UC-157**, from UC Riverside, is known for very high yield. Good choice for more mild coastal areas, as it tolerates warmer areas with mild winters.

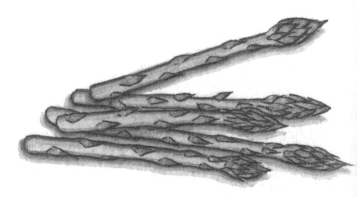

Basil

Basil is hot! It's the most widely used herb in the world and a favorite among edible landscapers. We knew there was a reason we loved it: from its beautiful (no, it doesn't only come in green) foliage to its fragrant flower, this brilliant culinary herb is a versatile addition to the landscape, with many very different looks. And hopeless romantics, take note: according to no less a man than Sir Thomas More, a man taking basil from a woman will love her always.

GROWING Do not plant basil until the daytime temperature is consistently in the 70s, and nights are above 50°F. Although basil prefers full sun, it grows reasonably well in part sun. Evenly spread organic all-purpose fertilizer in the garden before planting and mix the fertilizer into the soil. Add organic compost before planting, too. Basil grows best in a rich, well-drained soil, with a pH of 6.0 to 6.5. Plants need a relatively constant supply of moisture, so it is best to water by soaker hoses or drip irrigation.

Direct sow basil seeds as soon as the temperature remains between 60 and 80°F. Seeds should germinate in about 5 days at 70°F. Space plants approximately 12 inches apart. If using an intensive planting strategy, you may place the plants a bit closer, but maintain good airflow to prevent foliar fungal diseases. Basil plants should not be overfertilized; the flavor in the foliage is reduced during rapid plant growth. About 2 months after planting, basil may be fertilized again if plant growth is reduced and foliage color has become paler green. Phosphorus-deficient plants are usually dark green with reddish purple leaf tips and margins; correct with a blended fertilizer or bone meal mix. A liquid fish emulsion and seaweed product may then be used as a foliar feed. To reduce soilborne diseases, rotate herbs to different parts of the field each year and remove and destroy all plant debris after final harvest.

HARVESTING Begin harvesting leaves any time after plants have reached a height of 6 to 8 inches. For the most flavorful foliage, pinch out flower buds as soon as they appear. Pinch out terminal growth of the plants to encourage branching.

VARIETIES **Bush Basil** has small leaves and is more tolerant of different growing conditions. The lemon-scented **Lemon Basil** is generally a smaller, more compact plant. **Thai Basil**, with a slight licorice flavor and aroma, is used in many Asian dishes.

Beans

Common beans originated in the New World and were widely used by indigenous peoples throughout North and South America. Today, the most popular types with home gardeners are snap beans, romano or Italian beans, and lima beans. Each of these types divides further into two kinds: low-growing bush beans and tall-growing pole (or runner) beans. As a vertical grower, I prefer pole beans: these climbers give our hummingbirds a lovely drink, and their gorgeous blooms are stunning.

GROWING Beans require full sun for good growth and yield. They will not germinate well when the soil temperature is less than 60°F (70°F for lima beans). Optimum soil temperature is 60 to 77°F. Although they will grow in a wide variety of soils, a well-drained, friable (crumbly), sandy loam is best. Maintain a soil pH of 6.0 to 6.8. Apply 1 or 2 inches of water (adjust to current conditions) at weekly intervals, filling the root zone (mature rooting depth is 2 feet) at each watering and allowing the root zone to dry partially between waterings. Adequate moisture is especially important from flower bud formation to pod set. Beans grow poorly in wet or waterlogged soils.

Seed bush beans 1 to 1½ inches deep and 2 inches apart in rows spaced 15 to 18 inches apart; seed limas only 1 inch deep if soil is heavy and 4 to 6 inches apart. Seed pole beans 4 inches apart; space slender poles 12 inches apart. Beans are legumes and can produce some of their own nitrogen. To supplement this at planting, add a 10% organic nitrogen fertilizer. Excessive nitrogen can cause plants to produce large amount of leafy growth but fewer beans, so be careful not to overdo.

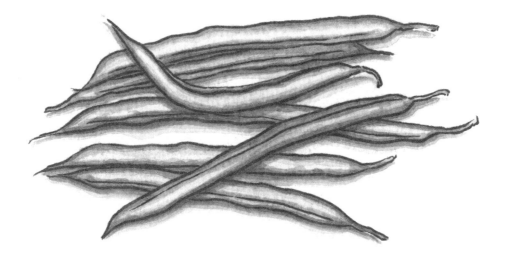

Cutworms and beetles are the major pests. Handpick or use organic insecticidal spray with pyrethrins if populations get out of control. To control fungal and soilborne bacterial diseases, rotate your planting site. Resistant varieties are the best defense.

HARVESTING For fresh use, harvest snap beans while the pods are slender, before they begin to bulge or yellow; harvest lima, shell, field, and soybeans when the pods are well filled. Dry beans (shell, field, and soybeans) should dry on the vine as long as possible (until the first heavy frost, if necessary) before harvesting. Pull the plants and leave them in the sun for 2 to 3 days to speed drying. A thoroughly mature bean is hard. Beans are easily canned, dried, or frozen. Store well-dried (and insect-free) beans in a can or jar with a tight cover (to keep out insects and rodents) in a cool, dry, dark place.

VARIETIES Bush: **Borlotto Bush** (aka **Tongues of Fire**) is popular in Italy. The beautiful white pods with flame-like red streaks make a great snap bean if harvested young, a good shelling bean, and a great baked bean. **Cranberry Shell**, a popular bean with chefs, can be harvested as a snap, shell, or dry bean. Maroon-colored beans have darker red and cranberry marking. This heirloom dates back to the 1800s and does well in short-season and cool-summer climates. Rich flavor is unsurpassed. Pole: **Blauhilde**, a spectacular purple climbing bean, is a German heirloom. Pods stay tender and stringless even at 10 inches long. A beautiful plant in edible landscapes. Blooms are rose-purple; vines climb to 9 feet; best used fresh; tolerant to mosaic virus. **Sunset Runner** is a wonderful climber for our vertical designs; it produces pretty peach blossoms and cascades of runner beans that can be delicious either as a young tender fresh or shelling bean.

Beets

Beets are easy to grow and another of our favorite "root to tip" vegetables, as both the root and the green tops are delicious and nutritious. The beautiful colors in their tops also make them wonderful visual elements in an edible landscape.

GROWING Beets perform well in full sun or part shade and grow best in the spring and fall. They require a well-draining sandy loam, high in organic matter, with a pH of 6.5 to 7. They do not tolerate acid soil. Beets require consistent moisture, so water deeply and thoroughly and do not let the soil become dry. Underwatering will cause the outer leaves to turn yellow and the roots to become woody; however, overwatering can diminish plant performance. Mulch after plants are established to help control soil moisture loss.

Typically better results are obtained by direct sowing rather than transplanting. Optimum germination temperature is 50 to 85°F (range is 40 to 90°F). Days to emergence: 5 to 8. May take 2 to 3 weeks in colder soils. Apply a fertilizer that contains both nitrogen and phosphorus prior to planting. Work the fertilizer into the soil as the seedbed is being prepared.

Flea beetles can be a pest for beets. Use insecticidal spray with pyrethrins if damage is extensive. Control fungal diseases by crop rotation, trimming infected leaves, cleaning tools, spraying with fungicide at first sign of disease, and good garden hygiene.

HARVESTING Begin harvesting when the roots are at least 1 inch and up to 3 inches wide. Beets tend to get tough if left to grow any larger. Harvest beet greens as you thin the seedlings and continue until the greens are too tough. Prepare the leaves as you would fresh spinach. Beet roots will keep in the refrigerator for up to 2 weeks.

VARIETIES **Detroit Dark Red** is early, very dark red, and very sweet. Grows to about 3 inches across. Bright golden roots and tender tops make the heirloom **Golden** a great salad beet, lovely in the garden and on the plate. The Italian heirloom **Chioggia** (aka **Candystripe** or **Peppermint**) has red and white concentric rings when cut. Root is early and sugary sweet. The leaves of **Bull's Blood** are an edible landscaper's dream—a strikingly deep, dark purple. This beauty is one you can grow in the garden during the summer, not for its root but for its tops. Root is a deep rich red, and delicious too. Often requested by chefs; heat resistant.

Broccoli

Spurned by generations of children who couldn't be convinced to "eat the tree"—no more! Broccoli is doing just fine, thank you very much. A third of American households are eating it at least once every 2 weeks, a 33% increase! And since a 2011 Georgetown University study found that isothiocyanates (phytochemicals found in broccoli and other cruciferous vegetables) caused cancer cells to die—well, let's just say broccoli is no longer the awkward kid no one talks to at the party!

GROWING This cool-season crop grows best in a sunny spot, with daytime temperatures of 65 to 80°F. Temperatures below 40°F will cause harm and possibly early bolting. Although broccoli will grow in a wide variety of soils, a sandy loam—reasonably fertile, well drained, moist, with plenty of added organic matter is best. A pH of 6.0 to 7.0 will cut down on clubroot and other diseases that plague this crop and keep nutrients available to plants. Broccoli requires regular watering; as always, a water-conserving drip system is best.

I prefer planting broccoli as a transplant rather than direct sowing. A good transplant is 5 to 6 weeks old, sturdy, with good color. Older plants or those that have already formed small heads won't yield as well as younger plants, so be selective at the nursery. Choose your planting time

carefully! Not too early. If you're planting from seed, sow seeds ¼ inch deep and space rows 24 to 36 inches apart, setting transplants or thinning seedlings 18 inches apart. In an intensive planting scheme, I place my plants 6 to 8 inches apart. If you added lots of good compost prior to planting, your soil should be adequately fertile come planting time. Side-dress with blood meal or spray with liquid fish emulsion as needed. Broccoli raab is a particularly heavy nitrogen feeder.

Flea beetles, root maggots, and caterpillars can cause serious damage to broccoli. Cover beds with floating row covers of spun-bonded polyester for the first month or more to prevent attacks by these pests. You can leave row covers on throughout the growing season, if necessary, or try an organic insecticidal soap for the soft-bodied pests. Use an insecticidal spray with pyrethrins on the beetles. Control fungal diseases by crop rotation, trimming infected leaves, cleaning tools, spraying with fungicide at first sign of disease, and good garden hygiene.

HARVESTING Remove broccoli heads by hand by snapping the stem and refrigerate immediately. Broccoli requires rapid cooling to ensure preservation of quality.

VARIETIES **Broccoli of Calabria**, a traditional variety from southern Italy, is early with a medium head; also vigorously produces tender side shoots. **Marathon Broccoli** is a late variety with a large head; highly tolerant to cold. **Sessantina Grossa Broccoli** is a 12- to 14-inch raab with a strong broccoli flavor that mellows with cooking. Forms more of a head than its cousins. Stems, shoots, buds, and leaves are edible.

Brussels Sprouts

Brussels sprouts are one of the more shade-tolerant edibles. They don't mind starting out in the warm days of the end of summer or fall, but do best when they develop flowers in cooler weather, so planning planting time is critical. A touch of frost actually sweetens the buds of this good-for-you vegetable.

GROWING Like most edibles, Brussels sprouts perform best in full sun; they tolerate light shade, but it will slow their maturity. A soil rich in organic matter with high moisture-holding capacity is necessary to keep the plants growing vigorously. Brussels sprouts demand a sweet soil, so be sure the pH is about 6.5. Keep soil evenly moist; fluctuations in moisture level during heading can cause developing sprouts to split and become bitter. The trick to watering Brussels correctly is to water deeply but infrequently.

Direct sow in August or September, or transplant nursery starts in October or November. Plant seed 3 to 4 inches apart, ¼ to ½ inch deep, in rows about 30 inches apart. Even though you start out with a good foundation of rich, fertile soil, Brussels sprouts will benefit from a balanced all-purpose fertilizer being added at planting time. Brussels sprouts must have a large amount of available nitrogen. Side-dress with an organic nitrogen fertilizer (blood meal) at least three times: the first, after the plants have been in the garden about 3 weeks, and then two more applications 2 weeks apart. Each application should be about 1 tablespoon per plant. To side-dress, make a shallow furrow with your finger around the plant, about 3 inches away from the trunk. Sprinkle the fertilizer into the circle and cover with soil. Water in well. Avoid applying additional nitrogen after sprouts are beginning to form to prevent loose and splitting sprouts.

Use a strong spray of water or a damp paper towel to wipe off cabbage aphids. For stubborn infestations, of aphids or other soft-bodied pests, use organic insecticidal soaps. Use insecticidal spray with pyrethrins to control beetles; handpick slugs and snails, or use an organic desiccant.

HARVESTING Before sprouts become crowded on the stem, break off the lower leaves over a period of a few weeks, starting at the bottom and working up the stem, leaving the uppermost leaves intact. Pick when sprouts are 1 to 2 inches in diameter and firm. Sprouts keep well at 32°F and high humidity for 6 to 8 weeks. The whole plant may be stored in a cool cellar and the sprouts removed as needed.

VARIETIES The compact heirloom **Long Island Improved** bears 50 to 100 sprouts. **Jade Cross**, a 2½-foot-tall hybrid, produces oval, medium-sized sprouts. **Falstaff** and **Red Ball** are dark purplish.

Cabbage

I love this plant! Not only is it nutritious and delicious, but its many varieties—with different shapes, sizes, colors, and textures—make cabbage a strong player in my edible landscaping plant palette. Don't limit this stunner to just the vegetable plot.

GROWING This cool-season (but frost-tender) crop grows best in a sunny spot, with daytime temperatures between 65 and 80°F. Some light shade is tolerated but slows growth. Although cabbage will grow in a wide variety of soils, a sandy loam—reasonably fertile, well drained, moist, with plenty of added organic matter—is best. The pH should be between 6.0 and 7.0. Cabbage requires regular watering; as always, a drip system is best.

Cabbage is easy to grow from seed. Start indoors during frost-prone times, as seeds need at least 40°F to germinate. Transplant when plants are 4 to 6 weeks old. Space plants at 8 to 24 inches, depending on the planting strategy you use and the variety you are growing. Having been amended with lots of compost prior to planting, your soil should be adequately fertile come planting time. Plants are heavy nitrogen feeders. Watch your cabbage carefully to determine when to add more fertilizer. Plants should be at least 6 inches tall before you fertilize them again (usually 8 weeks after planting). Add a nitrogen-heavy fertilizer (such as blood meal or fish emulsion). If using liquid fertilizer, spray the plot along the outer sides of the cabbage rows, about 6 inches from the plants.

Use a strong spray of water or a damp paper towel to wipe off cabbage aphids. Handpick caterpillars and destroy. Use insecticidal spray with pyrethrins to control beetles; handpick slugs and snails, or use an organic desiccant. Row covers may be useful on small plantings to help protect plants from early damage. Control fungal diseases by crop rotation, trimming infected leaves, cleaning tools, spraying with fungicide at first sign of disease, and good garden hygiene.

HARVESTING Harvesting at the correct time will depend on the variety, so know what you grow! Size doesn't always matter. Mature solid heads that are firm all the way through when squeezed indicates readiness. When ready to harvest, cut head at the lowest point possible. To store, place wrapped in plastic in the crisper section of your fridge. It should stay fresh for several weeks.

VARIETIES **Mammoth Red Rock** is a large heirloom with deep red heads. **Perfection Drumhead Savoy**, a large heirloom drumhead type, has finely savoyed leaves (crinkled) that are mild and sweet.

Carrots

Who doesn't have fond childhood memories of Peter Rabbit and Mr. McGregor's carrots? Carrots have been a food staple for most of us since before we could feed ourselves. No wonder we have nostalgic visions of the vintage garden filled with beautiful carrot tops peeking out of the soil.

GROWING Carrots thrive in the cooler moist conditions of early spring or late fall into winter. They grow best at 60 to 70°F; warmer temperatures early in the growing phase are fine, but they will suffer if temperatures drop below 50°F for long. Coastal areas can plant in fall, but inland valleys should not plant in hotter weather as carrots will grow very slowly, with poor results. Carrots grow best in a deep, loose soil that retains moisture yet drains well. Optimum pH range is 6 to 6.5. Root quality is best when soil temperatures are 60 to 70°F. Carrots need regular water to keep the top greens healthy, and it improves the quality of the harvested root. Plan on giving them an inch of water per week and keep soil evenly moist. Avoid extremes of either dry or wet soil, as large swings can affect root formation and taste.

Direct sowing is best. Spacing is usually 1 to 2 inches apart. Seeds germinate slowly. Proper soil preparation for this root crop is very important and should be done deeply to make sure the root zone soil is friable (crumbly); this ensures the roots can grow straight, without any obstruction. Amend your soil with rich fertile compost. As your carrots grow, make sure the tops of the roots are covered with soil. Plan succession plantings every 3 weeks through the cool season for continuous supply. Apply a balanced, all-purpose organic fertilizer when the tops are 3 to 4 inches tall and again when they are 6 to 8 inches tall.

Use floating row covers to protect plants from pests. For aphids and soft-bodied pests, use organic insecticidal soap. For other pests, handpick or spray with insecticidal spray with pyrethrins. If you plant disease-resistant varieties, practice crop rotation, and use drip irrigation and good garden hygiene, you shouldn't see any fungal diseases; if you do, spray with fungicides at first sign.

HARVESTING Carrots should be harvested when they are no more than 1½ inches in diameter, usually about 90 days after seeding. Having said that, it is entirely up to you as to how young you harvest. Carrots harvested smaller are prized by chefs and bring a whole different flavor profile to the plate. Smaller carrots should be used within a few days. Larger carrots will keep for a few weeks. Carrots can be canned, dried, or frozen.

VARIETIES Fast and easy to grow, **Nantes** is adapted to a range of climates and soils. A favorite of chefs, **Chantenay** develops stocky roots that become sweeter as the soil cools in the fall. **Danvers** makes great juice, and the sturdy roots store well, too.

Cauliflower

..

Yes, cauliflower is exacting in its climatic require-ments. It won't produce heads in hot weather and tolerates frost only as a mature fall crop. Most culti-vars need about 2 months of cool weather to mature, though some require as little as 48 days and others over 95 days. This is what makes growing cauliflower so challenging at the coast, especially when we have a warm autumn—but the sweet, mild taste of this home-grown brassica makes the challenge well worth it.

GROWING Plants like temperatures in the 60s and a moist atmosphere. It is crucial to keep soil evenly moist. Prepare soil ahead of planting time with plenty of organic matter (so that it will have a high capacity to hold a lot of moisture) or a pre-plant fertilizer high in nitrogen and phosphorus (16-20-0). Cauliflower demands a sweet soil, so be sure the pH is about 6.5.

Nursery transplants work just fine. If starting your own seeds, sow in containers 4 to 5 weeks before planting in the garden. Seedlings should be transplantable in 4 weeks. If you didn't use self-blanching varieties, wrap the outer leaves up around the developing florets and hold together with paper clips to shade them. Cauliflower is a heavy nitrogen feeder. Side-dress with an organic nitro-gen fertilizer (blood meal) at least three times. Make the first side-dressing after the plants have been in the garden about 3 weeks, and then two more applications 2 weeks apart. Each application should be about 1 tablespoon per plant. To side-dress, make a shallow furrow with your finger around the plant, about 3 inches away from the trunk. Sprinkle the fertilizer into the circle and cover with soil. Water in well. Avoid applying additional nitrogen after sprouts are beginning to form to prevent loose and splitting sprouts.

Common pests include slugs and snails, cabbageworms, stink bugs, aphids, and beetles. Use an organic desiccant for slugs and snails, an organic insecticidal soap for the aphids or other soft-bodied insects, and an organic insecti-cidal spray with pyrethrins on beetles or other hard-bodied insects.

HARVESTING Cauliflower will usually be ready for har-vest within a week or two after blanching. Keep an eye on it to avoid its becoming too mature. You'll want to pick the cauliflower once the head is full but before it has begun to separate, usually at about 6 to 12 inches in diameter. Cut the cauliflower from the main stem, but leave a few of the outer leaves attached to help protect the head's quality until ready to eat. Soak the head in salt water (2 table-spoons to 1 gallon) for about 20 to 30 minutes. This will help purge the cauliflower of any cabbageworms that may be hiding out inside the head. Cauliflower keeps best when frozen or canned, but it will keep for a week or so in the refrigerator if swaddled in plastic wrap.

VARIETIES **Snowball**, a self-blanching heirloom, pro-duces six to eight pure white heads. **Cheddar** produces heads about 4 to 7 inches wide and has 25 times the beta carotene of the regular white. **Graffiti** sets large heads of deep purple; the color intensifies with exposure to sun; perfect for coastal climates.

Celery

Are you of the mind that celery is the "empty vessel" of vegetables? Just a little chlorophyll, mixed with crunch and water? Well, I think celery deserves another look. Besides that no soup broth should begin without it, celery's a good source of vitamin C, potassium, and fiber, and it contains coumarin, an antioxidant that enhances the activity of white blood cells.

GROWING Place in a bright spot out of direct sun. Celery is very sensitive to early and late season frosts; optimum temperature is 70 to 75°F during the day and about 60°F at night. Celery prefers rich, fertile, well-drained sandy soil containing lots of organic matter and a neutral pH. Provide good drainage and air circulation, and plenty of water (1 to 2 inches a week). Celery has a shallow root system, so frequent, thorough watering is a must. Fluctuations in watering will have an adverse effect on the taste of the stalks. Drip irrigation is the way to go.

Nursery transplant stock is the easiest way to get started. There must be an abundant supply of nutrients in the shallow part of the soil for this shallow-rooted plant, so amend soil before planting: mix in a balanced all-purpose fertilizer, and integrate 2 to 4 inches of rich organic compost into the top layer of soil, to a depth of 6 to 8 inches. Planting 6 inches apart will help force tall straight plants. Apply a side-dressing of a complete balanced all-purpose fertilizer about 6 weeks after transplanting and apply a nitrogen fertilizer 4 weeks later.

Blanch celery stalks to keep them from becoming bitter. You can grow a self-blanching variety, or blanch conventional varieties. There are several ways to do this. One is to gradually pull the soil up around the plants as they grow, keeping the leaves exposed. Another is to tie the tops together 2 weeks before harvest, and mound soil up to the base of the leaves. Alternatively, cover the stalks with large cans (remove both ends first), drain tiles, or sleeves made out of paper or other material. Water carefully after setting up your blanching system so you won't wet the leaves and cause them to rot.

Use organic insecticidal soaps if you see aphids, or wipe them off with a damp paper towel. To keep diseases at bay, plant resistant varieties. Ensure good air circulation in your planting bed. Spray with fungicide. Do not overhead water.

HARVESTING Harvest outer stalks first, when they are 12 inches or taller. Whole plants can be harvested when they are 3 inches or more in diameter. The inner stalks (aka hearts) are the most tender and flavorful. Celery will keep in the refrigerator for up to 2 weeks.

VARIETIES **Golden Self-Blanching** is smaller in size and a faster grower than most; yellowish stalks. **Tango** is a self-blanching hybrid. **Red Celery** prefers cool moist weather. Beautiful red color; rich walnut flavor. **Tall Utah 52-70** has dark green stalks with a very compact habit; good winter celery.

Chard

Another boon to the edible landscaper, this beautiful leafy green is a delicious and interesting alternative to spinach and lettuce. Chard (aka Swiss chard) is available in a bouquet of strikingly gorgeous bright colors and features a mild, earthy flavor.

GROWING Chard prefers a sunny location (but will tolerate part shade) and the cool weather of early spring and fall (60 to 70°F). Plants are frost tolerant and may even benefit from a light kiss of frost, which makes the leaves sweeter. Leafy greens like chard grow best in well-drained soils, rich in organic matter. Loams generally produce the greatest yields; however, sandy loams are better for overwintering and spring crops. A soil pH of 6.0 to 6.5 is optimum. Leafy greens require rapid, succulent, continuous growth to achieve the best quality, so supply plenty of moisture and fertilizer. A steady supply of water is especially important. Insufficient moisture can result in tip burn, slow growth, and less flavorful leaves. Avoid wetting the plant when applying water, in order to avoid disease. If possible, irrigate with drip lines or soaker hoses. If using overhead (sprinkler) irrigation, water in the morning.

You can either direct sow or plant out nursery transplants. Optimum germination temperature is 85°F (range is 40 to 95°F). Sow seeds ½ to 1 inch deep, 2 to 6 inches apart. Side-dress with an all-purpose organic fertilizer when plants are 4 to 6 inches tall. Additional side-dressings of an organic nitrogen source, especially in sandy soil, may be needed.

Most diseases of chard are fungal. Keep them in check with good garden hygiene, crop rotation, cleaning tools, and good cultural practices; control their severity by spraying with fungicides at first signs and trimming the worst of the diseased leaves. Use an organic desiccant for slugs and snails and an organic insecticidal soap for aphids and other soft-bodied insects.

HARVESTING Like other greens, you can harvest chard at any size that suits your preparation and pleases your palate. The smaller the leaf, the more tender and mild-tasting it will be. If you take no more than 30% of the leafy canopy at each harvest, the plant will regenerate quickly. Store leaves in the fridge in ventilated plastic bags.

VARIETIES **Bright Lights** is a 20-inch plant with dark green, bronzed, wrinkled leaves. Stems, midribs, and secondary veins are gold, yellow, orange, and pink. Harvest baby leaves in 28 days. Makes a great and beautiful microgreen. **Fordhook Giant** is a compact plant with thick, dark green, wrinkled leaves with white veins and stems. Harvest baby leaves in 25 days.

Chives

....

Chives are smaller relatives of garlic, leeks, and onions and have a similarly fine, oniony flavor. Like all their family members, they are full of antioxidants and phytonutrients—the more pungent the flavor, the more powerful the health benefits.

GROWING Plant in a sunny location. Chives grow best in well-draining soil that is rich in organic matter and slightly acid (pH 6.2 to 6.8). Water regularly. Keep soil evenly moist. Chives are most often propagated by dividing the clumps in early spring. They can be grown from seed sown in spring, but seeds are slow to germinate and it can take 4 to 6 weeks to produce transplants. Also, seed-grown plants produce variations in leaf texture and size. I use nursery starts for the ease and consistency. If soil was amended before planting and compost is added routinely, supplemental fertilizing shouldn't be needed; however, plants that are harvested frequently benefit from supplemental fertilizer during the season. Be careful not to overfertilize, as this can interfere with flavor.

Control bulb mites, thrips, and other soft-bodied insects with organic insecticidal soaps. Fungal diseases can be avoided or controlled through good cultural practices—irrigating correctly, good soil management and garden hygiene, protective spraying with fungicides.

HARVESTING Begin harvesting chives about 30 days after planting. Cut the leaves down to within 2 inches of the soil. Cut from the outside of the bunch. Sharp scissors work best, as they won't damage the plant. Flowers, which are edible, appear in May and June. Store fresh herbs and flowers in a small cup with a little water. Chives do not dry well but can be frozen.

VARIETIES **Garlic Chives** (aka **Kow Choi**) has a mild garlic flavor.

Cilantro

Looking for a truly global herb? Look no further. Chinese parsley, coriander, cilantro—whatever you call it, chances are you will be using it no matter what cuisine you're cooking. Mexican, Chinese, Vietnamese, Thai, Indian, Moroccan, Caribbean—it's everywhere. Yet, cilantro is one of those herbs people either love or hate. There's even a Cilantro Haters club! Well, we love it around here, so we save a bit of space for it in our garden, always.

GROWING Cilantro loves sun but not heat. It will bolt in summer heat. Plant in a moderately fertile, well-draining, sandy loam with a pH of 6.5 to 7.5. Don't let newly planted cilantro dry out. The need for water reduces as plants become established. Take care not to overwater.

On the coast, cilantro can be planted year-round, but it definitely does best in spring and fall/winter. In the inland valleys, planting in the early spring and late fall is safest. If you want to try to grow it through the summer in the inland valleys, be sure to sow one of the slow-bolt varieties and give the plants protection against afternoon sun. Sow cilantro seeds ½ inch deep and space 2 inches apart if you are growing for the fresh herbs. For coriander seed, space the seeds 8 to 10 inches apart. If you love cilantro, you'll use a lot of it, so make sure you plan to succession sow for a continued harvest. Fertilize once or twice during the growing season by applying a foliar spray/drench of fish emulsion, or side-dress with ¼ cup of an organic nitrogen fertilizer (like blood meal) per 25 square foot of growing area. As you've learned, more isn't better when it comes to fertilizing, so be careful not to overdo. Too much nitrogen sacrifices taste.

Remove caterpillars and aphids manually; if populations are out of control, use insecticidal soap. To control soft rot and other fungal diseases, increase airflow, don't overwater, and use a fungicide.

HARVESTING Harvest cilantro leaves when they are about 6 inches long. If you are interested in harvesting the coriander seeds, wait until the plant has flowered and the seed heads turn brown. Place the seed heads in a bag and let them dry until the seeds fall off.

VARIETIES Leaf cilantro: **Santo** is the standard cool-season cilantro. Good for seed harvesting. **Culantro** (aka **Spiny Coriander**), used in Asian and Caribbean cuisine, grows best in shaded, moist soil. **Oaxaca** is a Mexican heirloom. Slow bolt: **Long Standing**, **Jantar**, **Vietnamese**, and **Leisure** grow happily in the warmer months.

Corn

Corn has deep roots, roots entwined so deeply in our collective ancestral memory that we can instinctively (and accurately) describe this crop as ancient. Perhaps this is why the image of corn fields waving in the breeze stirs feelings of connectedness—to heritage, home, hearth, and the "land o' plenty"—in so many of us.

GROWING Corn requires high temperatures for successful germination and growth; it does not tolerate cold weather, and frost will injure sweet corn at any stage of growth. Sweet corn grows best in well-draining, deep, naturally rich, loamy soil; it adapts to a wide range of soil pH, but best growth is at pH 6.0 to 6.5. For best germination, soil temperature should be between 70 and 85°F. Corn needs a continuous supply of moisture to ensure pollination and growth of kernels in the ear. After the tassels are produced, sweet corn requires 1 to 1½ inches of water each week. Irrigate with drip lines or soaker hoses for maximum efficiency.

Test your soil for fertility and amend for any deficiencies before you plant. Adding at least 3 inches of organic compost is always best. Sow corn 10 to 15 inches apart within rows, with each row about 36 to 42 inches apart. Plant several short rows rather than only one or two rows, for successful pollination and increased yields. After the plants are up, thin them to 12 inches apart. If planted too close together (less than 1 foot), the corn will have small, poorly filled ears. Side-dress with an organic high-nitrogen fertilizer like blood meal, starting when the plants are about 2 feet tall.

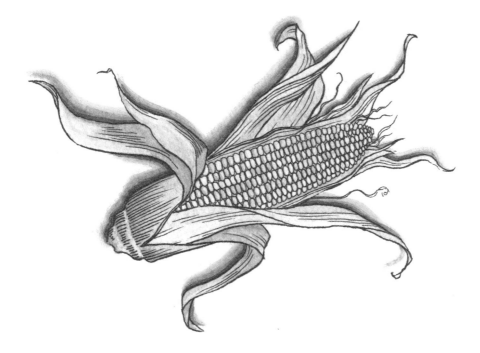

Common pests of corn include aphids, flea beetles, grasshoppers, spider mites, thrips, and birds. Insecticidal sprays with pyrethrins will take care of the hard-bodied insects. Insecticidal soaps give adequate controls for soft-bodied insects. Root rot frequently occurs on seedlings planted in cool, moist soil. Delay planting until soil temperatures are adequate to allow for rapid germination. Rust and leaf blights can be a problem in extended periods of warm, moist weather or areas of high dew point. Look for cultivars resistant to rust, or spray with fungicides.

HARVESTING Each sweet corn plant will produce at least one large ear that should be harvested at peak maturity, when the silks are dry and brown and the ear has enlarged to the point that the husks are full and tight. Sweet corn is best eaten immediately. Some gardeners actually bring the cooking water to boil before heading out to harvest! Storage life is 4 to 10 days at 40 to 45°F.

VARIETIES Many organic growers prefer the following cultivars. **Platinum Lady** and **Bodacious** are good early-season sweet corn varieties. **Silverado**, **Kandy Corn**, **Argent**, and **Snowbelle** are excellent mid-season varieties. **Delectable**, **Pegasus**, and **Silver Queen** are good late-season white corns. **Golden Bantam**, **Country Gentleman**, and **Stowell's Evergreen** are all heirlooms.

Cucumber

Whether for pickling or slicing, cucumbers are easy to grow and a "can't miss" in your summer garden! The vining types are terrific vertical growers: they save a ton of room in a garden plot (and they perform better) if you grow them up a support. Bonus: they'll do all the climbing themselves via their tendrils.

GROWING Give cucumbers full sun, sufficient moisture, and a well-drained, fertile soil, rich in organic matter with a near-neutral pH. Consistent, plentiful moisture is needed until fruit is ripening. May develop bitter taste if let to dry out. Do not plant until soil reaches 65°F. Cucumbers are very sensitive to cold, and planting in cold soil can prove disastrous. These days it is easier to find some of the less common varieties in some commercial nurseries; if you can find nursery stock, plant them! This will give you a considerable jump on the growing season. Direct-seed 1 to 1½ inches deep and 2 inches apart in rows. Do not overcrowd; these plants are susceptible to fungal diseases, so maintaining good air circulation is paramount. Cucumbers require periodic supplements of an organic fertilizer. Be on the lookout for pale, yellowish leaves, as this can indicate nitrogen deficiency. Leaf bronzing is a sign of potassium deficiency.

Cucumber mosaic virus is spread by aphids, so controlling their populations is critical. Plant resistant varieties, and use a strong spray of water early in the day or a damp paper towel to wipe off aphids. For stubborn infestations, of aphids or other soft-bodied pests, use organic insecticidal soaps. Use insecticidal spray with pyrethrins to control beetles. To control fungal diseases, space and trim plants to open up airflow. Plant resistant varieties. Spraying with a fungicide as a proctectant early is key, as is good garden hygiene, always.

HARVESTING My chefs prefer we harvest cucumbers on the smaller side. This provides a more tender skin and smaller seed cluster and lessens the chance of bitterness. Simply cut the cucumber from the vine with sharp harvesting scissors. Flowers too are edible, but remember that if you choose to harvest them, you'll be sacrificing production. Try keeping cucumbers in a cool spot in the kitchen (55°F) in perforated plastic bags. If that is not possible, store them for a few days in the fridge.

VARIETIES Vining: **Armenian** is actually a melon; its light green, mild-tasting, easily digestible fruits reach 24 inches long but are best harvested at 18 inches. The heirloom **Lemon Cuke** is the shape, size, and color of a lemon, but the taste is all cucumber. Chefs love this one. It pickles well. **Persian** is another favorite with chefs for its mildness, low seeds, small size, and edible skin. Makes awesome pickles as well.

Dill

A favorite herb of mine in my kitchen, I also love it for its ability to attract and sustain wildlife in my garden. It's one of those plants that practically flash an "Eat Here" sign to egg-bearing moths and butterflies. And in the love language of flowers, according to folklore, dill's "attribute" is lust.

GROWING Site dill in sun to part shade. As weather warms, it may need afternoon sun protection. Grows best in cool temperatures and in well-drained soil, pH 5.8 to 6.5. If you have heavy clay, don't even bother trying to grow this herb in the ground. Grow it instead in an outdoor pot at least 12 inches deep.

Dill is sensitive to three things: soil, heat, and transplanting. So prepare your soil well with lots of compost, grow dill only in the solidly cool seasons (late fall through early spring), and sow dill seeds directly. Succession sowing every 2 to 3 weeks will provide a continuous crop throughout the growing season. Germination occurs at 60 to 70°F; optimum soil temperature is 70°F. Sow seeds ¼ inch deep. Allow enough space between plants to allow for good air circulation. Keep soil evenly moist until established, then allow to dry a bit between waterings. Do not overwater. Dill does not require frequent fertilizing. A light feeding of an organic, balanced, all-purpose fertilizer applied once in late spring should be enough if soil was thoroughly amended at planting time.

Dill is a host plant for swallowtails and painted lady butterflies, to name a few, so whenever we can avoid using insecticides, we do. Wipe off aphids with a damp paper towel. Handpick cutworms and caterpillars. Following sound organic practice—soil maintenance, plant spacing, irrigation, good garden hygiene, trimming infected leaves, crop rotation—should help you avoid powdery mildew and other fungal diseases, as will applying a protective spraying of fungicide, renewed after a heavy rain.

HARVESTING Harvest just before you use it, as dill loses its flavor quickly. Cut stems down to about 2 inches above soil (the stems are tasty, too). If you need to store it in the fridge, place the bundle in a cup with a little water in it (don't let the leaves touch the water). It can easily be dried as well.

VARIETIES The popular **Bouquet** grows to about 3 feet. **Fernleaf**, a slow-to-bolt dwarf that grows only 18 to 24 inches, is great in small gardens and containers. The 2-foot **Super Dukat** is intensely flavored and slow-bolting. **Long Island Mammoth** is popular commercially. Plants are 30 inches tall and a good source of both leaves and seed.

Dragonfruit

Looking for a stunningly beautiful exotic of your very own? Well, have I got a fruit for you: dragonfruit (aka pitaya). After all, how can you resist the siren call of a fruit that was created thousands of years ago by fire-breathing dragons? Or so the story goes. The very sweet fruit, which tastes like a cross between a kiwi and a pear, is high in antioxidants. And the flowers are stunning!

GROWING The spined stems of this vining epiphytic cactus can grow more than 20 feet, and the plant will eventually need support on trellises 5 to 8 feet high. Plants are drought tolerant and cold hardy to 28°F, but cool weather slows down fruiting. Give dragonfruit well-drained soil rich in organic matter and full sun near the coast (it will need some sun protection inland). Apply a balanced all-purpose 6-6-6 type fertilizer every 2 months.

Dragonfruit grows slowly from seed. You can buy seeds already prepared, or you can get the seeds yourself from the fresh fruit. Plant the seeds shallowly in a well-draining potting soil, keeping the seed moist. Emergence should be in about 2 weeks. Pot up the seedlings and give them support as they grow. You can also propagate from cuttings, either rooted or directly planted. Using a 12- to 18-inch cutting is best. It takes 30 to 45 days for buds to mature and open, and another 45 days for fruit to develop. Plants are self-fruitful, but since they bloom at night (each flower for only one night) when very few pollinators are active, you may need to pollinate yourself. Plants have two or three flowering cycles. There are no major pests.

HARVESTING Unopened buds are sometimes cooked and eaten as vegetables. Cut fruit when it has a bright, evenly colored hot pink or reddish outer shell. Outer shell has large scales. Fruit should give a little bit under pressure.

VARIETIES **American Beauty** has rose-pink scales and deep pink flesh with a highly rated taste. **Delight** is light green with tinges of pink outside, with white-speckled flesh.

Edamame

I have to admit, these are like potato chips to me. The delicious simplicity of a bowl full of perfectly steamed edamame sprinkled with sea salt is perfection. The only way to improve on that picture of home contentment is to grow it yourself!

GROWING Edamame grows best in full sun but will tolerate some light shade. Plants perform well at temperatures around 70°F and in various soils, as long as they are rich in organic matter, but a light loamy soil is best. Soil temperature should be at least 60°F. Water needs are similar to green beans: keep the soil evenly moist; water stress at any point, especially from bloom to pod fill, can negatively affect yield. Nursery stock is usually available for this popular edible. If you choose to propagate from seed, sow at a depth of 1 to 1½ inches. Close spacing actually increases yields and shades out weeds. As a legume, edamame possesses that wonderful ability to fix nitrogen, so if you have amended your soil well, you shouldn't need to fertilize. If needed, side-dress with a balanced all-purpose organic fertilizer. Chlorosis (yellowing of leaves with green veins) is a symptom of iron deficiency; if this becomes a problem, fertilize with a chelated iron fertilizer.

This bush bean requires no support and is largely pest-resistant, but start with floating row covers to provide protection early on. Beetles and grasshoppers can usually be controlled by handpicking.

HARVESTING Watch for the beans swelling inside the pod. You'll have to keep a close eye on them to catch them at their peak. Being left on the vine too long results in a starchy bean. When you think they are close (beans are almost touching each other in the pod), you can pop one open to do a taste test. Sweet and tender is what you're going for. Beans freeze very nicely, so you'll be able to enjoy this snack throughout the winter.

VARIETIES **Beer Friend**, an early soybean, is a prolific and popular Japanese variety. **Korean Black** is a late soybean with a very sweet flavor. Can also be left on the bush to mature for dried beans. Seed coat is black with green interior. **Midori Giant**, an early traditional soybean, is a very heavy producer.

Eggplant

Grilled, fried, or baked, there's nothing like the flavor of fresh homegrown eggplant. These beautiful plants, with foliage from dark green to silvery olive, give us fruits in an array of jewel box colors. A joy to look at and a joy to eat!

GROWING This plant is very cold sensitive, requiring a frost-free period of 100 to 140 days. Requires 75 to 85°F days and nights above 65°F. Eggplants do best in well-draining soil that is rich in organic matter with a pH 5.5 to 6.5. Keep soil consistently moist, but once plants are established they can tolerate a bit of drought.

The smaller, slender eggplants are our favorites. We grow only these types for our chefs, who feel the traditional large eggplant has too tough a skin and too many bitter seeds. Good nurseries will carry a wide variety of eggplants, including the lesser known varieties of Japanese or Italian heirlooms, but as always, growing from seed really opens up a world of possibilities. Sow seeds ¼ to ½ inch deep in flats or seed pots filled with a rich soil mix. Optimum germination temperature is 70 to 90°F. Seeds usually germinate in 7 to 14 days. Once seedlings emerge, continue to keep the soil warm and moist, but not soggy. Transplant seedlings into prepared garden beds, spacing plants 18 to 24 inches from each other, in rows 30 to 36 inches apart. Although most plants are self-supporting, plants heavy with fruit benefit from some support. Side-dress with an all-purpose organic fertilizer when plants reach about half their mature size, and again when the first fruit is harvested.

Unfortunately, pests and diseases can be a problem. Use hoop houses while plants are small to protect them from pests. Control aphids and caterpillars by spraying with organic insecticidal soap. Spray with fungicide as a protectant against root rot and other fungal diseases. Practice crop rotation and good garden hygiene; maintain good air circulation.

HARVESTING Harvest when fruit is 4 to 6 inches long. Eggplants are ready when the flesh does not spring back when gently pressed. Cut the fruit off the plant with harvesting scissors.

VARIETIES **Casper** is a medium-sized ivory-white. **Fingers Mix** offers various slender eggplants in white, purple, and green. **Listada de Gandia** is a Spanish heirloom, bright purple with lovely irregular white stripes and sweet tender flesh.

Fava Beans

Forget what you've heard. Yes, if you harvest fava beans (aka broad beans) full size they can take a little more work, but did you know they can be eaten fresh, just like a snap pea, when you harvest pods under 4 inches in length? These younger pods can also be grilled and eaten whole (a trick I learned from a chef), and the delicious and tender young shoots of the plant can be used like a pea shoot, in stir fries, sautéed or tossed in a salad, or wilted in soup.

GROWING A cool-season annual, favas are generally planted in the fall or winter. They are frost resistant, but some varieties do not do well in the heat of the inland valleys, so time planting carefully in that region. Optimum growing temperature is 70 to 80°F. They grow best in well-drained, fertile, and friable (crumbly) soil, with a pH of 6.0 to 6.8. Apply 1 or 2 inches of water (adjust to current conditions) at weekly intervals, filling the root zone (mature rooting depth is 2 feet) at each watering and allowing the root zone to dry partially between waterings. Adequate moisture is especially important from flower bud formation to pod set. Beans grow poorly in wet or waterlogged soils.

Sow seeds 1 to 2 inches deep, spaced 6 to 8 inches apart, in regular garden soil. Legume inoculant is recommended for the initial planting. These are erect bushy plants, 4 to 9 feet tall, so place them in the back of the bed or use them as companion plants to shade tender vegetables. If wind is an issue, it is best to plant them against a vertical support that you can tie them to, securing them in a wind event. The flowers are edible and fragrant, a beautiful ivory with dark maroon throats. This multi-talented legume makes a great cover crop due to its fantastic ability to fix nitrogen. To supplement this, add a 10% organic nitrogen fertilizer at planting. Do not to overdo nitrogen.

Aphids are the only insect I've found to be an issue. I would not use the hose-off method, especially if you're growing in the coastal areas, as wet foliage can bring on fungal diseases. Instead, try to control manually by wiping them off young shoots with a damp paper towel, or spray with organic insecticidal soap. To control fungal and soil-borne bacterial diseases, rotate your planting site and practice good garden hygiene. Once plants fill in they will be very dense, so be vigilant about spacing and keeping good airflow between the plants and throughout the bed.

HARVESTING Size at harvest is up to you, depending on whether you're after shoots, young pods, or the beans themselves. Make sure to use the young shoots; the stems and leaves will become tough as they age. Fava beans usually take 3 to 5 months to be ready for harvest, although weather will have something to do with this. Be patient and watchful. If you wait too long to harvest the pods, the beans inside will be tough. Length of pod when ripe will depend on variety.

VARIETIES An old English favorite, **Broad Windsor** is an upright, 4-foot-high non-branching form with 5- to 8-inch-long pods and large beans. Very tasty. **Aquadulce** is an old variety, frost tolerant, 4 feet high. **Vroma** is heat tolerant, with large beans in 7-inch pods.

Fennel

All parts of this wonderful year-round perennial plant are usable: fronds, bulb—even its pollen. One flower can produce ¼ teaspoon of pollen, which can take up to an hour to harvest. No surprise, then, that this spice is so coveted and pricey—over $10/oz. Like saffron, it is very potent: a little goes a long way.

GROWING Plant in a sunny spot for best results, though fennel can take some light shade and even withstand light frosts. It does best when it reaches maturity in cool weather (90 to 110 days). Daytime temperatures should be 60 to 70°F. Fennel produces the best quality bulbs in a rich, well-drained soil, with a pH of 5.5 to 6.8. Keep soil evenly moist while plants are young; mature plants are drought tolerant.

I prefer growing fennel in the fall rather than in early spring, as it is very sensitive to day length and sudden chills. Our falls are tending to be warmer now, so I see more success when direct sowing in fall. Soil temperature should be 60 to 90°F for good germination. Leave plenty of room: bulbing fennel is a large plant. Nursery transplants are a simple way to get fennel into your garden fast and without too much of a challenge. Start to blanche the lower stems when the bulb is about the size of an egg by hilling up the soil around the bulb. About 3 weeks after that, bulbs should be ready to harvest. With a good start in well-amended, rich soil, fennel should need only a bit of a side-dressing with compost in mid-season.

Pests and diseases do not usually bother fennel. It is a host plant for swallowtail caterpillars, but even if multiple larvae are chewing away, they usually don't do enough damage to warrant destroying them. An occasional aphid or whitefly may show up, but a good spraying with insecticidal soap can control them. Root rot, the only disease that I've experienced, is usually due to overwatering.

HARVESTING Harvest bulbs when they get to about 3 inches in diameter. Any larger, and the plants will probably bolt and the flavor of the bulbs will suffer. Use a sharp knife or pruners to cut the bulb free right at the soil line. Trim the leaf stems 1 to 2 inches above the bulb to prepare it for storage. Bulb fennel will keep in the refrigerator up to a week. Stalks can be dried or frozen; leaves can be frozen or dried as herbs. Store dried leaves in an airtight container.

VARIETIES **Florence Fennel** is a bulbing fennel. **Sweet Fennel** is a seed fennel. Non-bulbing **Bronze Fennel** is the go-to plant for edible landscapers seeking to bring this beautiful color into the garden. Fronds are prized by chefs and mixologists.

Fenugreek

This native of southern Europe and Asia is one of the herbes du jour increasingly requested by chefs. Both seeds (the most commonly used part of the plant) and leaves have a slight maple scent and taste. The fresh leaves are tossed in salads; dried, they are used in teas and to flavor meat or poultry. Fenugreek has many medicinal qualities as well, being known as a cough and sore throat remedy.

GROWING Grow in spring in full sun to part shade. Fenugreek does not like cold and prefers well-draining, fertile, slightly acidic soil with a pH of 6.5. Amend soil with compost. Keep evenly moist but take care not to overwater: fenugreek hates waterlogged roots. Plants do not take well to being disturbed once germinated, so direct sow on an overcast day. In spring, sow seeds ¼ inch deep in a loose, loamy soil. Space plants 6 inches apart. Plants will reach 2 feet tall. If starting in amended soil, there's no need for additional fertilizing, as this plant has nitrogen-fixing capabilities. Amend soil in spring and fall to maintain fertility. Fenugreek actually thrives on benign neglect and is generally pest- and disease-free.

HARVESTING Harvest fresh leaves before the flowers form, about 6 weeks after sowing, by cutting the stem a few inches above the base of the plant when plants are about 1 foot tall. Harvest and dry seed pods in the fall. Store them in an airtight container.

VARIETIES Not usually offered in seed catalogs. Look for **Methi** (aka **Mathi**) in Asian markets. The most common of the two types are the large-seeded varieties, with slightly larger leaves and white flowers. If you're using the white-flowered type, you'll have to succession sow, as it will not regrow after cutting. Smaller forms with yellow flowers will regrow after cutting.

French Tarragon

French tarragon, one of the classic fine herbes *of French cuisine, is an essential aromatic herb and a chef's best friend. It has a unique anise flavor that's subtle but distinctive. Lemony, with a hint of licorice—more delicate than fennel—it's bright-tasting without being overpowering. Every chef we grow for asks to include this herb in their garden each spring and fall.*

GROWING Grow this cool-season perennial as an annual in warm areas, in sun to part shade. French tarragon is sensitive to heat but quite drought tolerant once established. It prefers a well-draining soil, pH 6.5; soil should be loose and enriched with organic matter, which makes it easier for the plant's shallow, fleshy root system to penetrate. Flavor is intensified when plants are grown in nutrient-poor soils, so fertilize only when planting. Nursery transplants are easiest; after that, plants are best propagated through root division.Water needs are average; let soil dry out between watering. Plants are susceptible to whiteflies. Use insecticidal soap to control.

HARVESTING Harvest the leaves and flowers as needed. While best used fresh, tarragon can be frozen or dried.

VARIETIES The true **French Tarragon**, indigenous to Russia and western Asia, has the "purest" flavor. **Russian Tarragon** is less flavorful but more robust, growing to a height of about 5 feet. **Mexican Tarragon**, a perennial with small golden flowers in the fall, can easily take the place of the longed-for French tarragon in our kitchens. It too has a wonderful anise/licorice scent and taste.

Garlic

Where would we be, culinarily speaking, without garlic? There are two types: hard and soft neck. Hard neck is preferred by many chefs for its pungent, earthy flavor but doesn't grow well in dry, hot weather. Soft necks tolerate more heat.

GROWING Grow garlic in full sun. Garlic does best when planted in rich, loose, fertile sandy soil, with a neutral pH. For hard necks, fall or winter planting is the preferred timing to harvest in spring or early summer, before warm weather hits the inland valleys. Soft necks tolerate warmer weather (as in the inland valleys) and so can be planted a bit later, in the fall or spring. Don't skimp on amendments: garlic demands high fertility.

Get seed garlic that is certified organic and disease-free from reputable sources. Separate the bulbs into cloves and plant each clove pointed side up with ½ to 1 inch of soil above them. Before planting, dig a balanced fertilizer containing phosphorus and potassium into the soil; this provides the nutrients plants need initially to form strong roots. Later, when the leaves are 4 to 6 inches tall, give garlic plants a dose of nitrogen, such as manure, blood meal, or fish emulsion, to boost leaf development. Once bulb formation starts, do not use a nitrogen fertilizer, as this can lead to bulb rot. This and other fungal diseases can be avoided or controlled with good soil management, garden hygiene, and cultural practices, including irrigating correctly and using protective fungicides before fungal issues are seen.

HARVESTING First harvest is in early spring when plants are about 1 foot tall. This is when you can harvest garlic "green"; its mild garlic flavor is highly prized by chefs, who use the young immature bulbs like scallions. Second harvest is of the scapes (round stalk), which appear around mid-June. Snap scapes off when they curl. They are delicious, mildy flavored, and also a big chef request. The removal of the scapes will also concentrate the plant's energy into bulb formation. The main harvest is in late July. Reduce irrigation for the month leading up to harvest to lessen the chances of bulb rot and to develop the paper skins, which will harden during the curing period. Watch the green leaves of the garlic. When the bottom three or four are dead and the top five or six are still green, it is time to dig up the bulbs. Do this with care: any nicks or injuries to the bulb prevent good curing and promote rot. Store bulbs in a cool, dry, shaded place. Brush off dirt and trim roots to ¼ inch and place apart on a drying screen with a permeable surface, to allow for airflow. Cure for 2 weeks, then cut the leaves off.

VARIETIES **Purple Italian** is a hard neck with a delicate and sweet spiciness. Another hard neck, **Spanish Roja**, is a favorite of chefs. Flavor is strong and spicy but not the hottest. Doesn't store long. Needs a cold winter, so should do better in the inland valleys. **California Early White** is great for the beginner. Flavor is hot but not the hottest. Early maturing and performs in most climates. Very prolific.

Grapes

This heat-loving deciduous perennial vine produces the fruit we love in late summer and fall. But first things first: whether you want grapes for wine or the table, you should work out your long-term plans for the support of the vines before planting.

GROWING Grapes need full sun, at least 8 hours a day. Insufficient light will impact fruiting and promote diseases. Less fertile, rocky, well-draining soils are actually preferred for wine production. Table grapes produce the preferable larger berries in deeper, richer soils, but the added fertility might promote vegetative growth at the expense of yield. Drought tolerant once established. Vines do not tolerate wet feet, so drainage is key. Install drip or sprinkler irrigation, and put down a 2- to 4-inch layer of mulch around the trunk (leave about 6 inches around trunk bare) to reduce evaporation. Once fruit sets, maintain an even moisture level to avoid cracking of fruit.

Grape vines can be purchased either bare-root or as 2-year-old vines in nurseries. Bare-root plants are more economical, but buying the 2-year-old plants will give you earlier fruiting, as grapes do not fruit fully until after their second year. Amend soil with compost if you are planting in poorly draining or sandy soils to improve texture, and follow all bare-root planting guidelines (see February's Skill Set). Plant 2-year-old vines at the same level or deeper than the surrounding soil. Form a well around the vine, and flood to ensure roots are wetted. If roots are circling or otherwise bound up, unravel them as much as you can and orient them downward and outward. If planting a grafted vine (unusual from nurseries), make sure the graft is well above the surrounding soil level. Place a 6-foot stake next to the

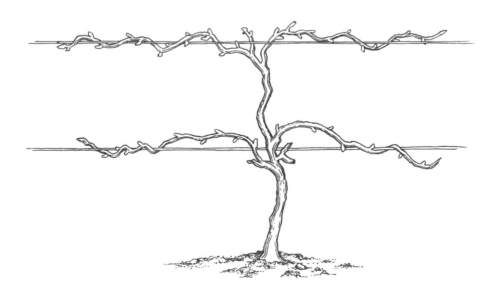

newly planted vine for temporary support for the vines. Nitrogen fertilizer should be used sparingly as an ongoing application, unless a deficiency has been indentified. An application of an organic nitrogen source (blood meal or fish emulsion) in January or February should prepare for good vine development in spring. If your target product isn't the grapes but the leaves (I have a chef who uses only the leaves), then a focus on nitrogen fertilizing is fine to promote leaf production instead of fruit.

Likely soft-bodied pests (ants, thrips, spider mites) can be controlled with organic insecticidal soaps. Watch out for fungal diseases (powdery or downy mildew, blight, leaf spot), particularly when the canopy is crowded. Do protective spraying with copper fungicides, especially at the coast in the spring and after heavy rain.

HARVESTING Harvest clusters when grapes are full size and sugar is fully developed. You can take tastes tests regularly throughout the summer and harvest when it suits your taste. Fresh grapes should be used right away. They can also be dried for raisins.

VARIETIES **Red Flame** is a medium-sized red grape, round, seedless. **Red Globe** is a very large red grape, round, seeded. **Thompson** is a medium to large green grape, cylindrical, seedless. All are table grapes.

Kale

* *

Most greens prefer the cool weather of early spring and fall, but this cold hardy, cool-season, A-list leafy green is also tolerant of hot summer weather. Kale tastes best with a bit of cold weather, even a frost. In fact, in many areas, kale will overwinter with protection, and it can be grown year-round on the coast with some afternoon sun protection.

GROWING Kale enjoys full sun in cooler months but tolerates, even prefers, part shade, especially in the hotter months. It grows best in well-draining soils, rich in organic matter, pH of 6 to 6.5. Loams generally produce the greatest yields, but sandier loams are better for overwintering and spring crops. A steady supply of water is important for good plant growth and quality. Insufficient moisture can result in tip burn, slow growth, and less flavorful leaves. If possible, irrigate with drip lines or soaker hoses. If using overhead (sprinkler) irrigation, water in the morning.

The more common kales are readily available in local nurseries. You may need to grow the less common varieties from seed. Germination temperatures range from 45 to 85°F (some germination can take place at 40°F). Plant seeds ¼ to ½ inch deep and 1 inch apart, and thin to 12 inches apart with rows 18 inches apart. This is standard spacing; however, you may choose to space them closer together if you're following a dense planting strategy and harvesting often. Assuming that you've started with good soil rich in organic matter, you should not need additional fertilizer until the plants are 4 to 6 inches tall. At that point side-dress with a nitrogen organic fertilizer like blood meal. Additional periodic side-dressings of an organic nitrogen source, especially in sandy soil, may be needed.

Kale is a trouper, but be on the lookout for cutworms, cabbageworms, and aphids (handpick or use an organic insecticidal soap) and snails and slugs (handpick or use an organic desiccant). To avoid disease, try not to wet the plant when applying water. A good crop rotation plan can keep rots and other fungal diseases in check.

HARVESTING Harvest kale at any time, at any size. Younger leaves will always be more tender than older leaves. Use microgreens and the smaller leaves raw in salads and as a garnish. The larger, tougher leaves benefit from high-heat roasting, long braising, and other robust cooking techniques. Kale will keep in the fridge for 10 to 14 days.

VARIETIES **Winterbor**, **Redbor**, and **Dwarf Blue Curled** are beautiful, heavily curled standard varieties that are more cold hardy. They make the most delicious roasted kale chips. The heirloom **Red Russian** has lovely serrated leaves with a purple rib and veins. **Nero di Toscana** (aka **Lacinato**, **Black**, **Dinosaur)** is a dark purplish Italian heirloom, a favorite among chefs for its flavor and texture. Not as cold hardy as Red Russian.

Leeks

As far as I'm concerned, leeks are a necessity in any serious cool-season culinary garden. Certainly, there is hardly a European garden without a gorgeous blue-green stand of leeks in winter. In SoCal and everywhere else in the United States, however, the leek remains underappreciated. From the edible landscaper's perspective, it provides a productive upright, structural element that broadens our design palette with its coloration (white to blue-green to dark green and even purple). From a chef's perspective, leeks are an integral ingredient, lending their elegantly delicate flavor to sauces, soups, and myriad other dishes.

GROWING Along with kale, leeks are the most cold-tolerant of vegetables. If established in late summer, they can overwinter through the frozen ground and snowpack. In fact, the colder the temperature, the sweeter the taste. On the other end of the spectrum, they will survive (but are not at all fond of) temperatures consistently above 85°F. Leeks are shallow-rooted crops that tolerate a wide variety of soil textures; however, dense clay soil or rocks can hinder growth and development. To provide ideal conditions, most garden beds will need at least 2 inches of compost mixed into the soil. A soil pH of 6.0 to 7.0 is optimum. Keep soil moist but not soggy, and allow it to dry out somewhat between waterings. If possible, irrigate with drip lines or soaker hoses. If using overhead (sprinkler) irrigation, water in the morning.

Grow leeks, which can take up to 5 months to mature, like long-season onions. They are better transplanted than direct sown. Growing them from seed takes patience and persistence (c'mon, we've got plenty of that—we're gardeners after all!), and germination can be a difficult. Sow seeds directly into your garden bed (½ inch deep, ½ inch apart, in rows 1½ to 2 feet apart), or plant seeds in containers and transplant seedlings into your garden. Seedlings are transplantable when they are 10 to 12 weeks old, with a stem ¼ inch in diameter. The size you choose to harvest your leeks will determine your spacing: leave more space in between plants that you intend to grow to a 3- to 4-inch width. In my small-space gardens (and combined with the fact that most of my chefs prefer their leeks with a diameter of 1 to 2 inches), I can get away with planting mine closer together. Leeks grown in compost-enriched soil will not need additional fertilizer. If you wish to fertilize, use a liquid kelp or balanced organic fertilizer 3 weeks after planting. Stop fertilizing 6 to 7 weeks before harvest. Be sure to hill up soil around the base of the leek to blanch as they grow.

Leeks are virtually bulletproof when it comes to pest and disease problems, but try not to wet your plants when watering, for extra insurance.

Leeks, continued

HARVESTING Harvest leeks when the bulb is at least 1 inch in diameter. Don't look for the flags (leek leaves) to turn brown as a cue: they stay green. Harvesting is all about size. Most of my chefs prefer to use them on the smaller side. Certainly, in my smaller gardens, harvesting them at a smaller size makes perfect sense. Use a spading fork to loosen the ground around the leeks, then gently pull them from the garden. Leeks will last longer if left in the ground until ready for use. Once harvested, they can be stored in the refrigerator for several weeks.

VARIETIES **American Flag** (130 days), pure white blanched stems with mild sweet flavor and good winter hardiness. **Bleu de Solaise** (105 days), French heirloom with blue-green to almost blue foliage tinged with red. Extremely cold hardy with fat, succulent shanks. **Broad London** (120 days), very squat, short-shanked (4 to 6 inches), sweet, creamy-textured old variety. Some heat tolerance and moderate cold tolerance. **Giant Musselburgh** (150 days), German heirloom, pure white, sweet, tender, short-shanked, dark green foliage. Unfortunately, with rare exceptions (see Resources), U.S. seed catalogs carry only a few varieties of leeks. Northern European seed companies offer greater diversity.

Lettuce

Lettuce is one of those vegetables where there is a huge difference in taste between homegrown and store-bought. An added bonus: it is one of the easiest things we can grow! Lettuce is a cool-season edible, but it is possible to extend the harvest with bolt-resistant/heat-tolerant summer varieties.

GROWING Site with some thought to both sun and wind protection, as both can harm lettuce. It is not just a matter of too much exposure to intense sun that is the problem; it is the heat index (the combined effect of temperature and humidity) as well. While we can do things to control the former using some kind of shelter, we can't do much about the latter. As the weather warms, you must start paying attention to the heat index. NOAA tracks this, and it is easy to look up online. As you watch the heat index and temperatures rise, it is time to switch to heat-tolerant varieties.

Lettuce does best in humus-rich, moisture-retentive, well-draining soil with plenty of nitrogen-rich organic matter. Leaves turn bitter quickly if the plant is allowed to dry out. While it is always best to water in the mornings, lettuce may need a refreshing little afternoon shower as well. As the weather warms, you may notice that your lettuce leaves are wilting, even collapsing. If a quick check of the soil reveals appropriate moisture, plants are suffering from heat stress. Set your hose attachment to the misting setting and give your lettuce bed a little spritz, but don't do this too late in the day, as the leaves need time to dry off before nighttime.

To sow lettuce directly in the garden, plant the seeds

about ¼ inch deep and water gently. Space the seeds according to the packet instructions. Remember, some rules are meant to be broken, so harvesting a head lettuce like a leaf type is A-OK if the taste and form please you. Succession sowing is a perfect strategy to keep you in salads every night. Sow seeds every 2 weeks or so. Lettuce craves two things: water and nitrogen. If you start with richly amended soil, your lettuce plants are off to a great start; however, depending on how densely you're planting and how aggressively you harvest, supplemental side-dressing with an organic nitrogen fertilizer might be necessary. A dry organic fertilizer like blood meal or fishmeal is a good, if slow-acting choice. If a faster-acting fertilizer is needed, a foliar feed of fish emulsion will do the trick. Don't overdo though, as excessive nitrogen will affect the taste of your lettuce.

Common pests include slugs and snails, caterpillars, and aphids. Use an organic desiccant for slugs and snails and an organic insecticidal soap for the aphids, caterpillars, and any other soft-bodied insects.

HARVESTING Lettuce is the most turgid (plumped up with water) in the morning, so that is the optimum time to pick it. Always taste as you harvest, so that you can gauge when the flavor profile is becoming bitter. Clear cut for heading varieties: use sharp harvesting scissors to cut heads below the lowest leaves, leaving about an inch of the crown behind. The plant will regrow in a few weeks. You can also pull plants out by the roots to keep the head intact. Harvest leaf types as needed by cutting the outside leaves, leaving the crown intact. Lettuce is best when eaten fresh but will keep up to 2 weeks when refrigerated.

VARIETIES The possibilities are almost endless, but here are some of my favorites. **Boston** (aka **Bibb**) is a head lettuce with a mild, sweet flavor and pale green leaves. **Red Sails** can be treated as either a leaf lettuce or a head lettuce. Beautiful ruffled red-maroon leaves. Crisp and sweet. **Oakleaf**, a leaf lettuce with a mild flavor, comes in green and red varieties. **Lollo Rossa**, a leaf lettuce, comes in reds and greens; loose rosette form with a bolder, slightly bitter but nutty taste.

Okra

Okra. It's not your grandmother's slimy side dish anymore. Chefs have rediscovered and rethought this beloved vegetable of Southern, Indian, Caribbean, Creole, and Cajun cooking. And it gets better: okra is an absolutely gorgeous plant with a spectacular flower—a star in the edible landscaper's playbook.

GROWING Okra does best in full sun, in well-drained, sandy soils that are high in organic matter, but it can be grown in average soils. Prefers a pH of 5.8 to 6.8. Optimum growing temperature is 70 to 80°F. Plants will tolerate some drought, but moisture is important during flowering and pod development. Irrigate with drip lines or soaker hoses.

Don't plant until soils have warmed up to at least 65°F at a 4-inch depth. Sow seeds directly into the garden. To improve germination, soak okra seeds in water overnight before sowing. This is a tall plant, so place it where its height can be used to shade more tender plants. Space rows 3 feet apart; sow seeds 1 inch deep and 4 to 6 inches apart within the row. Start with healthy fertile soil that has been amended with plenty of compost. Additional fertilizing shouldn't be necessary until the plants are 6 to 8 inches tall and again 2 to 3 weeks later. Take care not to overuse nitrogen, since it can cause excessively leafy growth at the expense of fruiting.

Use insecticidal spray with pyrethrins to control beetles and other hard-bodied insects. Good cultural practices, including crop rotation and protective sprays of fungicides, should keep southern stem blight and other fungal diseases under control.

HARVESTING Okra is ready to harvest when pods are 2- to 3-inches long, usually 60 to 70 days after planting. At this stage the pods are still tender; any larger, and pods will become too tough. Okra grows very fast, so harvest every few days to keep the plant in peak production. Handle the pods carefully—they bruise easily. Okra can be stored in the refrigerator for about 7 days.

VARIETIES Both **Burgundy** (beautiful burgundy-red pods) and **Clemson Spineless** (dark green pods) are open-pollinated heirlooms. **Cajun Delight** is a hybrid with dark green pods.

Onions

The foundation ingredient for most any dish, onions (including scallions and shallots) should be present and accounted for in any self-respecting edible garden—or kitchen. These are essential, and the variety you can grow at home beats supermarket offerings hands down. Additionally, their health benefits range from reducing inflammation to helping to regulate blood sugar.

GROWING Onions perform best in light, richly fertile loamy soil that is well draining. They do not tolerate water stress, so do not let the bulbs dry out. Consistent irrigation is best. Simply put, onions grow their tops in cool weather and form bulbs in warm, so it's best to plant onions in cool weather. Plant in spring except at the coast, where they do best as a late fall/winter crop. Make sure temperature doesn't go below 20°F. For sets or transplants (separate before planting bulbing onions), plant the smaller sets 1 inch deep, with 4 to 5 inches between each plant if you're growing the onions as bulbing onions but much closer if growing as scallions (bunching types can be planted closer together as well). Side-dress onions when plants are 6 inches tall, continuing every few weeks until bulb begins to swell. Stop fertilizing when bulbs are developing, as excessive feeding will result in lush tops and underdeveloped bulbs.

Onions are generally pest- and disease-free, but you may see onion maggots. Intercropping really helps to control this pest. Good crop rotation will help avoid disease problems.

HARVESTING Once onion tops turn yellow, use your feet or the back of a rake to bend them over horizontally. This diverts the plant's energy into the maturing bulb. When the tops turn brown, gently lift the bulbs and leave them to dry in the sun on dry ground, or dry indoors in a single layer for several weeks. Do not pile them on top of one another: they might mold, especially if there is any humidity. When the outer skins are thoroughly dry, wipe off any soil and remove the tops (unless you intend to braid them). Stored in a cool (40 to 50°F), dry place, bulbs will keep for 4 to 12 months.

VARIETIES In SoCal, the best onion to grow is the short-day onion, which forms bulbs when day length is 10 to 12 hours long. **Yellow Granex** (aka **Vidalia**) is my favorite! Very sweet. **White Bermuda** is extremely mild but has a short storage life, so it's great to grow as scallions or for eating raw (yes, we do that! think of Persian food). **Yellow Sweet Spanish** is a large onion with mild sweet flavor. All are short-day.

Oregano

Some folks go for the intense herbaceous flavor fresh oregano adds to chicken, vegetables, and pasta dishes, but most people agree that this Mediterranean herb tastes better dried. What would pizza or lemony Greek sausages be without it? It's essential in many Mexican dishes as well.

GROWING Oregano grows year-round in full sun. It withstands a moderate freeze and tolerates a variety of soils (as long as those soils are well drained) but grows best in a gravelly loam. Like most Mediterranean-type herbs, oregano needs only moderate water. In fact, just about the only way to fail is by overwatering. I prefer starting with nursery transplants, since I don't usually need more than one potent plant per garden. If you're growing from seed, you can direct sow in the late spring. As long as soil is amended with compost at planting and routinely during the year, oregano should not need any supplemental fertilizing. Control aphids and spider mites with insecticidal soap. Rust and root rot are mainly caused by overwatering. Fungicides can be tried, but once the disease is active they have little effect.

HARVESTING Begin harvesting oregano when the plant's stems are about 8 inches long. The flavor is most intense just before the plant blooms. Harvesting often produces a bushier plant and keeps foliage healthy and succulent. Easily dried.

VARIETIES **Mexican**, hot, spicy, and pungent—perfect for Mexican dishes. **Greek**, hot and peppery, with white flowers; extremely drought tolerant. **Golden**, bright yellow-green leaves and milder flavor.

Parsnips

My personal favorite, this root is a staple of my winter menus. Whether added to my mashed potatoes or in my slow-simmered stews, this vegetable brings with it a surprising amount of sweetness and never fails to build that umami (sweet and savory) flavor profile that elevates any dish.

GROWING Parsnips prefer full sun (but will tolerate part shade) and require a long, cool growing season. Optimum growing temperature is 45 to 75°F, but plants will tolerate cold and freezing temperatures. Like other root vegetables, parsnips require loose, loamy soil that is free of rocks and other debris that would inhibit the long, straight growth of the root. Optimum pH is 6.0 to 6.8. Prepare planting beds by adding plenty of rich compost. Parsnips require evenly moist soil for roots to develop well; as roots approach maturity, reduce irrigation to avoid cracking.

Direct sowing is the preferred method of propagation because, like other root vegetables, parsnips don't transplant well. Direct sow seeds ½ inch deep and 3 to 4 inches apart in late fall. In case of a hard frost in the inland valleys, place a layer of straw about 6 inches thick over the plants. Starting with well-amended soil is critical, but an additional side-dressing of compost mid-season will reinvigorate the soil for the growing plants. Given proper conditions (appropriate irrigation, exposure, etc.), parsnips are not usually bothered by pests or disease.

HARVESTING Parsnips are ready to harvest 100 to 130 days after sowing. Lift parsnips with a spading fork or gently pull them out of the soil, being careful not to damage roots. Leave parsnips in the garden as long as possible or until you need them, as exposure to cold temperatures develops the root's sweetness.

VARIETIES **All American** (105 days), sweet, tender heirloom, 2 to 3 inches across and 12 inches long. **Gladiator** (110 days), sweet taste, 7 inches long. **Lancer** (120 days), very sweet, uniform root.

Peas

These cool-season edibles can be harvested 11 months of the year, growing into the late spring in coastal areas with some afternoon sun protection, and all but guaranteeing that your pasta is never without its piselli. What's more, as legumes, peas possess the nitrogen-fixing quality that is so prized by gardeners. A caveat: proper drainage is a must, as peas will not thrive otherwise.

GROWING Peas grow best in cool weather and should be planted in early spring or late summer. The ideal temperature for growth is 55 to 65°F. Young pea plants can withstand a little frost, though frost may damage the flowers and pods. As a winter crop, peas tolerate temperatures down to 28°F. The best soil for peas is rich, loamy, and well draining (I cannot emphasize this enough). Peas are fairly sensitive to soil acidity; the optimum pH is 6.0 to 7.0. Like most edibles, peas can require up to an inch of water a week, depending on the stage of development. Although they should never be waterlogged, peas should never be allowed to dry out, especially when the plant is germinating or blooming, or fruit is setting and swelling. Garden peas and snow peas have both climbing and low-growing varieties. Sugar snap peas grow on tall vines that require the support of a trellis.

Peas grow better when you direct sow. Sow seeds about 1 inch deep and 2 inches apart in the row. Climbers need 3 feet between rows, or plant a double row 6 inches apart on either side of trellis; if you're using a biointensive strategy, you can plant much closer together. Add a little organic all-purpose fertilizer when plants are about 2 inches tall. Since legumes are very efficient at converting nitrogen in the soil, you shouldn't need to fertilize with nitrogen again unless, after pods begin to form, the plants appear yellowish or are not growing well. Crop rotation of peas and beans in the garden is crucial to reduce the incidence of soilborne diseases, which can build up over time.

HARVESTING Harvest garden peas when pods are well filled but still have that bright green color. The raw peas should taste sweet. Harvest lower pods first. Consistent daily harvesting increases production. Harvest snap peas before they touch each other in the pod for the sweetest flavor and crunchiest texture; the older the snap pea, the sweeter—up to a point. Peas are best when used quickly after harvesting, but they can be refrigerated in plastic bags and will keep for 2 to 4 days. Both garden peas and snap peas can be frozen, canned, or even dried. Snow peas or sugar peas have edible flat pods and very small seeds. They should be picked when very young, just as the seeds start to form. If not picked at this stage, they can be shelled and eaten as garden peas, but are more starchy and not as sweet. Sugar snap peas are also an edible pod pea but have larger and sweeter seeds and a thicker pod. Grow to full size and eat like snap peas.

VARIETIES Garden peas: **Tall Telephone** and **Lincoln** (good heat resistance) are both tall heirlooms. **Little Marvel** is an early dwarf variety. Sugar snap peas: **Sugar Snap** (the original) and **Sugar Ann** (dwarf). Snow peas: **Mammoth Melting Sugar** (reliably disease-resistant), **Dwarf Grey Sugar**, and **Oregon Sugar Pod**. **Usui** is a snow pea cultivated especially for its exquisite shoots—a favorite of many of my chefs.

Peppers

We eat with our eyes. It's a given. So imagine—where would our culinary creations be without the flavors and colors of the pretty pepper? An essential ingredient in my summer edible landscapes, these beauties can be sweet or hot, small or large, and very, very colorful in all their parts—flowers, fruit, and leaves!

GROWING These tropical plants thrive when temperatures are warm. Ideal temperatures are 70 to 80°F during the day and 60 to 70°F at night. Plants grow best in warm (60°F), well-drained soils of moderate fertility and good tilth. Peppers are not particularly sensitive to soil acidity, but best results are obtained with a pH of 6.0 to 6.8. Keep soil evenly moist. Reducing irrigation at time of fruit development can enhance flavor of some varieties, and for centuries, growers have increased the heat of chili peppers by slightly drought-stressing plants after fruit set. My experience has been that different varieties respond differently; I find fairly predictable responses from drought stress in jalapenos and serranos.

Traditional advice is to space plants 18 inches apart in rows 24 inches apart. As a biointensive planter, I space mine much closer together and have never had a problem (typically 6 inches apart for smaller types, 10 to 12 inches apart for larger). Once fruits have begun to set, apply a side-dressing of low-nitrogen fertilizer to promote productivity. Do not overfertilize with nitrogen, as that will have the opposite effect. Control aphids, thrips, and whiteflies with an organic insecticidal soap, and flea beetles with an organic insecticidal spray with pyrethrins. Reduce the occurrence of fungal diseases by maintaining good airflow, practicing crop rotation, and by watering early in the day so leaves dry well before evening.

HARVESTING Sweet peppers are normally harvested in the immature green stage (but full size) for use in relishes and salads, for stuffing, and for flavor in many cooked dishes, but if you allow them to ripen on the plant, they will be sweeter and higher in vitamin content. Other peppers are usually harvested at full maturity. Know the specific harvesting size and color of the varieties you are growing. Be careful when picking peppers, as the plant's branches are easily broken. Use hand clippers or pruners to avoid breaking the stem. Cool (45 to 50°F), moist conditions and high humidity are the ideal storage conditions for peppers. In general, they keep only 1 to 2 weeks.

VARIETIES Try **Fresno, Jalapeno, Anaheim, Serrano, Shishito, Pasilla,** and **Golden California Wonder**.

Potatoes

Potatoes are America's favorite and most popular vegetable—and that's not just because the USDA measures consumption by the pound. They are the very definition of comfort food, and healthful, too (they are very high in vitamin C and potassium). So mash them, bake them, boil them, hash brown them— just don't ever eat green potatoes!

GROWING Potatoes do best in cool regions. In warmer climes, flowering and vegetative growth suffers and is sometimes completely suppressed. Optimum temperature for growth is 75°F or lower. Potatoes tolerate light frost and a wide range of soils (except poorly draining), but they do best in a deep, loose, moist, sandy loam that is rich in organic material. They will grow successfully in a wide range of soil pH, but potato scab can occur if the pH is above 5.3. Plant potatoes in fall when soil temperature is 45°F.

I have found that planting in raised beds is easiest and provides the greatest yield. I use the hilled row method, keeping the soil that I remove to create the trenches in a small trash can that I keep nearby. Dig straight, shallow trenches, 2 to 3 feet apart, in heavily amended soil (lots of compost!). Plant seed potatoes 12 inches apart and cover with about 3 inches of soil. When the shoots reach 10 to 12 inches tall, use a hoe or shovel to scoop soil from between rows and mound it against the plants, burying the stems halfway. Repeat as needed through the growing season to keep the tubers well covered, as light develops the compound solanine to a potentially toxic level and turns the

potato green. Potatoes love fertile soil, so make sure you start with well-amended soil. Add a balanced all-purpose organic fertilizer to the planting bed. Be careful not to over-fertilize: this will produce lots of leaves, but tubers suffer.

Manually remove aphids with a damp paper towel or use an insecticidal soap. Control beetles with an insecticidal spray with pyrethrins. Both late blight and early blight are common in home gardens. Of the two, late blight is the real threat. Buying potato seeds from reliable sources, spraying with a protective fungicide, pruning carefully, and practicing good soil management and garden hygiene will help keep it from getting out of control.

HARVESTING Dig potatoes on a dry day. New potatoes will be ready for harvest 10 weeks after planting. Otherwise, wait until the vines have died before starting to harvest. If a hard frost is predicted, immediately harvest whatever potatoes are ready. Be very careful when harvesting not to bruise or nick your potatoes. Make sure you brush off any soil clinging to them, then store them in a cool, dry, dark place. The ideal temperature for storage is 35 to 40°F.

VARIETIES **Kennebec** has some resistance to late blight. **French Fingerling**, a chef favorite, has yellow flesh with an interior ring of red. **Yellow Finn** has a buttery sweet flavor.

Radicchio

....

These salad greens are a staple in our fall restaurant gardens and growing in popularity in our home gardens and edible landscapes as well. They are gorgeous to see in their full colorful glory—and it's so fun to watch them slowly develop that stunning color as the weather cools.

GROWING Frost tolerant: the colder it gets, the more radicchio's beautiful colors deepen. All grow best in cool weather. Plants are normally grown in spring or fall, preferring loose, well-drained soil with a high amount of organic matter. Ideal pH is 6.0 to 6.5. Soil temperature should be 50 to 72°F. Like lettuce, radicchio is shallow-rooted, so keep soil consistently moist and never let the plants dry out. Irrigate 1 to 1½ inches per week. Consistent moisture is especially critical about 2 weeks before heads mature.

Nurseries usually have some selection of radicchio on their shelves, but starting from seeds will give you so many more options—do try the lesser-known varieties! Seeds sprout in 2 to 15 days, depending on conditions. Sow seeds ¼ inch deep. If growing for full-sized heads, give them some room, about 4 to 6 inches between plants. Timing is everything with these plants: hot weather will quickly turn radicchio bitter, so mind the weather forecasts. I don't attempt these in SoCal until it's almost winter, as the weather in fall can still be too hot. In years that we have cool springs, I also plant in early spring. Just be ready to give the plants some sun protection if the weather warms. A rapid and consistent growth rate is critical to good head formation and yields, so make sure your soil is well amended with rich compost and add a balanced, organic all-purpose fertilizer at planting time. Do not add excess nitrogen, as this will interfere with the head formation and may cause premature bolting.

HARVESTING Harvest radicchio leaf by leaf or as a full-sized head. Size at harvest is entirely up to you and your taste: young, small heads are less bitter and more tender than full-sized heads. Heads are ready for harvesting when they're firm to the touch (usually after 60 to 65 days). To harvest, cut the entire plant just above the soil line. When stored in the refrigerator in a perforated plastic bag, heads typically last 3 to 4 weeks.

VARIETIES One of the most popular with chefs, **Treviso** is a beautiful classic Italian, with upright form and red and white stripes. **Castelfranco**, another chef and gardener favorite, has a colorful round head that features red and light green markings. An easier variety for beginners, **Chioggia** is a lovely, very consistent radicchio; it has dark red outer leaves with white markings.

Rhubarb

Everything old is new again. Thanks to renewed attention from chefs and mixologists, rhubarb is enjoying a comeback of sorts, but there seems to be a bit of controversy about whether or not it can be successfully grown here in SoCal. Well, I'm here to tell you—I've been growing it for years at our urban farm in Venice, with great results. So I say, "Yes, you can!" Both the inland valleys and coastal regions should give this vintage plant a try.

GROWING Proper siting is critical. You can count on rhubarb being around 5 to 10 years or even longer, but it doesn't transplant easily, so be certain about placement. Find the coolest but still sunny spot in your garden, and give this large plant some room (4 × 4 feet). Rhubarb is actually tolerant of most soils but is happiest in very fertile, well-drained soils that are high in organic matter. Prefers a slightly acid pH of 6.0 to 6.8. Keep soil evenly moist throughout the growing season. In inland valleys, give plants some sun protection: rhubarb becomes dormant as temperatures warm, and temperatures below 40°F are required to stimulate regrowth. Though our coastal temperatures don't drop that low usually, you may be able to find a suitable microclimate on your site. Growth in spring will continue as long as temperatures remain below 90°F. Rhubarb is drought tolerant once established.

Starting from seeds is not something I recommend, as it takes so long. Transplants are readily available seasonally; if you don't see them, talk to your nursery manager to see if they can order some for you. If not, rhubarb roots can be ordered online, usually in early spring. Rhubarb is relatively free of pests and disease problems, but do be sure to keep your bed routinely amended with compost. Rhubarb especially loves manure (we use a compost mix that contains chicken and bat manure). A side-dressing of about a cup of a balanced organic all-purpose fertilizer each spring is very effective.

HARVESTING Do not use leaves: they are toxic. Do not harvest stalks during the first year: the plant needs its energy to become properly established. Harvest stalks lightly the second year and as needed in the third year and beyond. Harvestable stalks are 12 to 18 inches long. Cut stalks as close to the crown as possible without injuring it. Stop harvesting when growth slows down and stalks get shorter and thinner. This is when the plant is storing up energy for next year's growth. Rhubarb freezes well.

VARIETIES **Victoria**—the best cooking rhubarb by far. It is sweeter and milder than all others, and I have had good results with it in carefully selected sites at the coast and inland. **Crimson Red** is similar but a better performer in inland valleys, as it is very winter hardy; choose the coolest site in landscape and provide some sun protection in the summer.

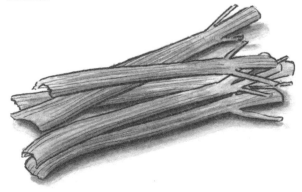

Strawberries

Ahh, strawberries. There's probably no other berry flavor so likely to stir childhood memories, from first trips to the strawberry patch to shortcakes, milkshakes, and ice cream cones. Lucky for us in SoCal, we can start planting these delicious, healthy berries as early as January and enjoy the harvest bounty for 10 months of the year!

GROWING For optimum fruiting, choose a well-drained location in full sun. Strawberries are shallow-rooted and grow best in sandy loams; the soil should be well supplied with humus and have a pH of 6.0 to 6.5. Plants require a relatively constant supply of moisture, especially as they become established. Water freshly dug plants intensively for the first week. Potted plants require less watering to establish. Both strawberry pots and raised beds are great ways to plant.

The matted row system is another great way to "grow" because such plantings may bear fruit for more than one season if properly renovated. Set the mother plants 2 feet apart, then let runners fill the bed the first summer. Remove flowers that first year, so no fruit is produced. Thin the plants, leaving only the most healthy and vigorous. Plants should be about 6 inches apart in all directions. Apply organic matter in the fall. If new plants appear light green and do not grow well, side-dress with a organic nitrogen fertilizer about a month after planting.

Phosphorus-deficient plants are usually dark green with reddish purple leaf tips and margins. Side-dress with bone meal to correct the problem.

Common pests of strawberries include slugs (try an organic desiccant) and aphids, thrips, whiteflies, and other soft-bodied insects (try an organic insecticidal soup). Good garden hygiene (cleaning tools as you work, trimming and collecting infected plant debris and leaves) can help keep fungal diseases under control.

HARVESTING Pick the strawberry with about one-quarter of the stem attached. The best time to pick is early morning, when berries are still cool. Not all berries ripen at the same time; pick only berries that are fully red. Strawberries are extremely perishable and keep refrigerated for 5 to 7 days, max.

VARIETIES Short-day (June-bearing) varieties (**Chandler**, **Camarosa**, **Sequoia**) start forming flower buds as the day length gets shorter and temperatures get cooler; these essentially produce in the late fall, winter, and especially in early spring, when days are short. Everbearing varieties (**Quinault**, **Ozark Beauty**) produce two crops, one in June or July and another in the fall. Day-neutral varieties (**Selva**, **Muir**, **Irvine**) are insensitive to day length and produce throughout the season as long as nighttime temperatures do not drop below 60°F. For optimal performance, the high-yielding Selva should not be planted before 10 September.

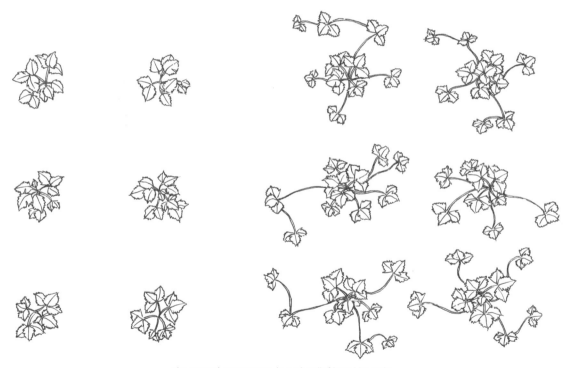

The matted row system, in spring (left) and by early summer, before thinning (right)

Thyme

Thyme is the most versatile herb in the edible garden, and shade-tolerant to boot. And don't forget: it's just one of the many herbs that are turning up fresh, by sprig or by the fistful, in celebratory "garden to glass" drinks. With thyme, you can even use the flowers. Try thyme in martinis and peach-flavored cocktails, like a Bellini.

GROWING Thyme does best in dry, loamy soil, rich with organic material, in full to part sun. A neutral pH is fine, but it performs better in slightly alkaline conditions. Water moderately: thyme doesn't like wet feet. Nursery stock is best for planting. After the first year, lightly prune back by one-third. Do not cut into the woody part. Do this each spring. This will keep the plant vigorous and keep it from getting woody. Pinching the tips occasionally will keep the plant full and bushy. Does not require much fertilization if soil's organic matter is routinely renewed. Side-dress with a balanced, organic all-purpose fertilizer in spring. Thyme is relatively pest- and disease-free. Spider mites can become a problem when the weather is dry; use insecticidal soaps to control populations. Apply a protective spraying of fungicide, renewed after a heavy rain, to reduce damage from root rot and other fungal diseases.

HARVESTING You can begin to harvest sprigs 1 to 2 months after planting. Simply snip sprigs as needed. Plants respond well to frequent cutting. Thyme is easily stored, whether dried, refrigerated, frozen, or preserved in oil or vinegar.

VARIETIES **Orange**, small-leaved with a definite citrusy orange-peel scent and flavor. **Lemon**, small-leaved with a strong lemon scent and flavor; in demand by chefs and mixologists. **Italian** (aka **Pizza Thyme**) has deep green oval-shaped leaves. **Caraway**, as its name suggests, has a pungent, anise-like flavor.

Tomatillos

Living in SoCal, we are greatly shaped by the cultures around us. For many of us, that means Mexican or Latin cultures. The music, the history, and the food are all inextricably part of the SoCal experience, and it shows up in our tastes and our gardens, too. If you are a fan of salsa verde, chili verde, or green enchilada sauce (to name just a few), you need tomatillos in your garden.

GROWING Give these frost-sensitive plants a hot spot in full sun, in moderately rich, loose, well-draining soil. Best growth occurs at temperatures above 65°F, but hot temperatures during flowering can result in poor fruit set. Tomatillos are very sensitive to wet feet. Although they can be moderately drought tolerant, tomatillos perform best if soil is kept evenly moist, especially during flower production and fruit set. Drip irrigation systems are best.

Start tomatillos indoors in early spring. Make certain to harden off your indoor starts before transplanting into the garden when soil is completely warmed up. Like their cousins tomatoes, tomatillos sprout roots along their stems, so they too prefer a deep planting. Be sure to give tomatillos plenty of space, as these very prolific plants can get 3 to 4 feet wide and tall. They will need a trellis for support. Tomatillos are lighter feeders than tomatoes. Usually, good soil preparation, with a couple of inches of rich compost, provides enough fertility for the growing season.

A great plant for beginners, tomatillos are rarely bothered by disease or insect pest problems. Cage the plants off the ground to allow air to circulate—which protects them from diseases, such as early blight—and to keep them out of the reach of slugs and snails.

HARVESTING Harvest should come at 75 to 100 days after transplanting. Pick the fruits when they fill out their husks, and the husks just begin to split. Don't harvest unless the husks are filled, but harvest before they turn pale yellow, as they become seedier and their flavor declines. Harvested tomatillos can be stored in their husks at room temperature for up to a week or in the refrigerator for up to 3 weeks.

VARIETIES **Toma Verde**, a standard type with large fruit, is very early, at 60 days after planting. **Purple** (65 days), an edible landscaper's choice for its beautiful color, has small but intensely colored fruit; long storing.

Tomatoes

There is a reason these jewels are the most popular edible grown in America: a fresh-picked homegrown tomato beats supermarket offerings every time for taste. And they're something of a seasonal timepiece, too. It just isn't summer until you see your 'mater vines starting to ramble up the trellis.

GROWING Tomatoes need heat and light to mature into ripe, flavorful fruits, so grow them in full sun. Temperatures of 65 to 75°F are optimum for plant growth. Tomatoes demand loamy soil that drains well and is richly amended with organic matter. A pH range of 5.5 to 6.8 is best, as is evenly moist soil. Large fluctuations in irrigation can lead to fruit cracking, blossom end rot, and other problems.

There are two types of tomato plants, determinate and indeterminate. The vines of determinate varieties grow only 1 to 3 feet long. Basically this type gives one large harvest all at once and then stops, which is a good solution for canners and gardeners with short seasons and small spaces. Indeterminate tomatoes can have huge vines that grow 6 to 20 feet long. They keep growing and producing unless killed by frost, disease, or lack of nutrients.

Cool-tolerant (aka early season) tomatoes perform well in temperatures as low as 55°F and usually mature within 52 to 70 days, faster than their peak-season siblings. Most (not all) are determinate varieties. Some are blight-resistant hybrids (Early Girl, Legend, Siletz, Oregon Spring), but most are heirlooms that hail from places (e.g., Russia, Czech Republic) with colder climates, higher humidity, and fewer daylight hours: Anna Russian, Black Krim, Caspian Pink, Cluj Yellow Cherry, Early Wonder, Galina's Cherry, Glacier, Gold Dust, Japanese Black Trifele, Jetsetter, Nepal, Orlov Yellow Giant, Paul Robeson, Polar Baby, Purple Bumble Bee, Purple Russian, Siberian, Stupice, Sunset's Red Horizon, Sub Arctic, Svetlana Red, Taxi, Tim's Black Ruffles. As the cool season advances, use season-extending systems like greenhouses and row covers to get the best-tasting harvest possible.

By planting healthy nursery stock, you are getting your tomato season underway that much sooner, and (unless you've settled on some very rare tomato seed that you simply must have), you will probably be satisfied with the huge array of tomato varieties available from commercial nurseries. Tomatoes love to be planted deeply. Dig a deep planting hole. Set the transplant in the hole so the lowest set of leaves is at soil level; fill the hole with a mixture of compost and soil. Gently press the soil down to ensure that there are not large air gaps and the root ball has made contact with its new soil. Water in well. Well-amended soil will have all the necessary nutrients and trace elements that tomatoes need until the plant is blooming and fruiting. As with all fruiting plants, applying excess nitrogen can produce beautifully leafy plants at the sacrifice of the fruit, so do not overapply.

Unfortunately, unless bred to be resistant, tomatoes are susceptible to many pests and diseases. For brevity's sake, I'm listing only the most challenging here. For caterpillars (including the dreaded tomato hornworm), flea beetles, and stink bugs, handpick or use an organic insecticidal spray with pyrethrins. Prevent and control late blight and other fungal diseases through solid soil management, good garden hygiene, and proper crop rotation, plant spacing, and irrigation.

HARVESTING Learn the mature size and color of the tomato you're growing. Once tomatoes start ripening (watch both color and size), check the vines daily to harvest at peak. Ripe tomatoes smell earthy and sweet and should give just a little with slight pressure. Tomatoes can easily be preserved through canning, pickling, and drying, spreading the homegrown tomato flavor into the next season. Never, ever store tomatoes in the refrigerator—it makes the tomato mealy and less flavorful. Instead, store them on your counter, stem side down. This keeps the bottom from rotting too quickly.

VARIETIES **Sungold**, yellow cherry, very sweet and dependable. **Sweet 100**, red cherry, very sweet and disease-resistant. Heirlooms: **Kellogg's Breakfast**, a beautiful orange beefsteak, very flavorful and sweet. **Brandywine**, large pink fruit. Wins prizes for taste! *And* for having moderate resistance to blight. **Green Zebra**, green-striped fruit. Mild flavor, excellent fresh or canned. All are indeterminate.

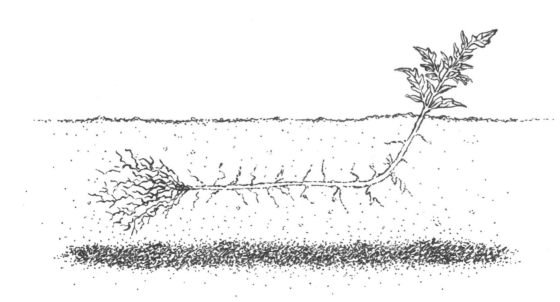

Deep-planting a tomato

Turnips

Root vegetables in the garden really signal winter to me. Gets me thinking of pulling out my slow cooker and starting the long parade of one-pot wonders. Turnips and other roots can almost take center stage here, as they develop their lovely creamy texture and sweetness during the low and slow of braises.

GROWING Turnips thrive in cool temperatures. Hot weather makes the leaves tough and the roots woody and bitter. Temperatures of 50 to 70°F encourage rapid growth and a high-quality crop. Light frost improves flavor, but plants won't tolerant hard freezes. Turnips prefer well-drained, fertile soil high in organic matter, pH 6.0 to 7.5; they will tolerate average soil, but poor soil will slow growth and diminish quality and flavor. Keep the soil evenly moist, as the root needs plentiful, consistent moisture.

As with all root vegetables, propagating by seed is best. Germination temperatures range from 45 to 85°F. Prepare soil deeply to remove any obstructions that would prevent the root's forming correctly. Sow seeds ¼ to ½ inch deep, 1 inch apart, in rows 4 to 6 inches apart. Thin plants to 4- to 6-inch spacings. Succession sow every 2 weeks for continuous harvest. Apply a mulch at least 2 inches thick when plants are 5 inches tall to insulate and retain moist soil. No extra fertilizer is necessary in well-prepared soil, and diseases usually aren't a problem if turnips are grown in rich, fertile, well-drained soil and harvested young. As for pests, use a hard stream of water to remove aphids from plants early in the day, or wash them off with a damp paper towel. Handpick any caterpillars, and use an organic desiccant for slugs and snails. Row covers may be useful on small plantings to help protect plants from early damage.

HARVESTING Harvest when weather is cool for best quality and flavor. Harvest roots when they are 2 to 3 inches in diameter, which is when they'll be the most tender. Harvesting on the smaller side gives you the option to enjoy the roots and tops either raw or cooked. If you have larger turnips, use them in soups, stews, and braises. To store the roots, remove tops (which you can eat), leaving half of the stem. Do not rinse soil off the roots. They can be stored as is in a root cellar or cool, dark pantry. Turnips are great pickled!

VARIETIES **Scarlet Queen** has crisp white flesh and lovely scarlet skin. Resistant to downy mildew. **Golden Ball** has yellow flesh and skin. **Gilfeather**, with green and white skin and cream flesh, tastes like rutabaga. Turnips for greens: **Alltop**, **Seven Top**.

Watermelon

"Mornings, before daylight, I slipped into corn-fields and borrowed a watermelon." **Yes, there's nothing like a little bit of Mark Twain,** Huckleberry Finn, **and some watermelon to get you thinking about summer and all the new adventures you'll have! But why borrow a watermelon when you can grow one (or several!) yourself? It's easy, here in SoCal.**

GROWING Watermelons grow best at average temperatures of 70 to 85°F, on a deep sandy loam that is high in organic matter, well drained, and slightly acidic (although plants take a pH range of 5.5 to 8.0). Watermelons need a lot of water, especially during fruit set and development: water stress during early development can result in small, misshapen fruit. When watering, make sure the soil is moistened to a depth of at least 6 inches. Avoid drastic fluctuations in soil moisture, as heavy irrigation (or rainfall) can result in fruit splitting.

Except for the bush types, watermelon vines require a lot of space. The soil temperature at the 4-inch depth should be 60 to 65°F before sowing; melon seed does not germinate well in cold soil. Plant seed 1 inch deep in hills spaced 6 feet apart. If you're using bush types, you can plant a bit closer together. When seedlings are established, thin to the best three plants per hill. For earliness, you can start sowing seeds inside about 3 weeks before you anticipate setting plants out in the garden; plant two or more seeds in 3-inch-deep pots or peat pots, then thin to the best two plants. Watermelon has moderate nutrient requirements compared with other vegetable crops, and thanks to its deep roots, it efficiently pulls nutrients from the soil. Side-dress before the vines start to "run" with a calcium-rich organic fertilizer (such as fish emulsion). Side-dress a second time after bloom, when fruit is developing.

Aphids transmit mosaic virus to the plants, and spider mites can cause severe reduction of yields. Use floating row covers, or spray plants with organic insecticidal soap. If you plant disease-resistant varieties, practice crop rotation, maintain balanced soil fertility, and use a drip irrigation system and good garden hygiene, you should be able to manage powdery and downy mildews and other fungal diseases.

HARVESTING Several things will tell you your watermelon is ripe and ready to harvest. The curly tendrils and leaves on the stem near the melon usually turn brown and dry. The melon's surface color dulls, and the bottom of the melon (where it lies on the soil) turns from light green to yellowish. The rind will be rough to the touch, and harder to penetrate with your thumbnail.

VARIETIES **Little Baby Flower**, a petite, pink-fleshed variety, ripens quickly and weighs in at just 4 pounds. **Sugar Baby**, my favorite of the small watermelons, doesn't get any bigger than 13 pounds and has been called an icebox watermelon, as it fits nicely into the fridge. **Jubliee**, a super-sweet variety developed in 1963, can weigh as much as 45 pounds, which classifies it as a giant.

Zucchini

For me, the SoCal summer isn't quite here until I see my workhorse of the garden, zucchini, in its full splendor of production. And produce it does! Two plants should be enough to feed a family of four (some would say an entire neighborhood), including oodles of zucchini bread. Let's get started—summer won't wait!

GROWING Zucchini plants need at least 8 hours of full direct sunlight a day. Temperatures over 70°F are favorable for growth and development, and plentiful and consistent moisture is needed from the time plants emerge until fruits begin to fill out. Soil should remain moist, drying slightly between waterings, but it should never be allowed to dry completely, nor should it remain too soggy. Plants prefer well-drained, fertile, loose soil, high in organic matter, with pH of 6.0 to 7.5. When zucchini is planted in compost-rich soil where nutrients are released slowly, additional fertilizers may not be required. An organic liquid fertilizer such as fish emulsion may be applied at 2- to 3-week intervals where soil isn't as fertile. Avoid high-nitrogen fertilizers; they will only encourage more leaves and stems.

Seed germination requires a minimum soil temperature of 60°F. After the danger of frost has passed, seeds should be planted to a depth of 1 inch. Generally plants are spaced at a minimum of 3 feet from center; however, in biointensive gardening situations this can be reduced to 1½ to 2 feet between plants. Common pests are aphids, spider mites, and whiteflies; control with insecticidal soap. Common diseases include bacterial wilt and downy and powdery mildew; control or prevent with proper watering (drip), good air circulation, and other good cultural practices.

HARVESTING For the most tender produce, harvest zucchini at their immature stage, when the rind is soft and seeds are underdeveloped. Fruits should be 6 to 8 inches long and 1½ to 3 inches in diameter. Be sure to cut the fruit from the plant at the stem between the fruit and the main stem. Squash blossoms too are edible and can be served raw or cooked. Harvest only the male blossoms, unless the goal is to reduce production, but always leave a few male blossoms on the vine for pollination purposes. Use pruning shears or a sharp knife to cut squash blossoms morning to midday when the petals are open, leaving 1 inch of stem. Gently rinse in a pan of cool water and store in ice water in the refrigerator until ready to use. The flowers can be stored up to 1 or 2 days. Although zucchini is best eaten when fresh, it can be canned or frozen. Freshly harvested produce can be refrigerated up to 2 weeks. Frozen zucchini lasts about 3 months.

VARIETIES **Black Zucchini** (best known; greenish black skin, white flesh), **Black Beauty** (slender, with slight ridges, dark black-green), **Cocozelle** (dark green overlaid with light green stripes; long, very slender fruit), **Vegetable Marrow White Bush** (creamy greenish color, oblong shape), and **Gold Rush** (AAS winner, deep gold color, superior fruit quality) are all open-pollinated.

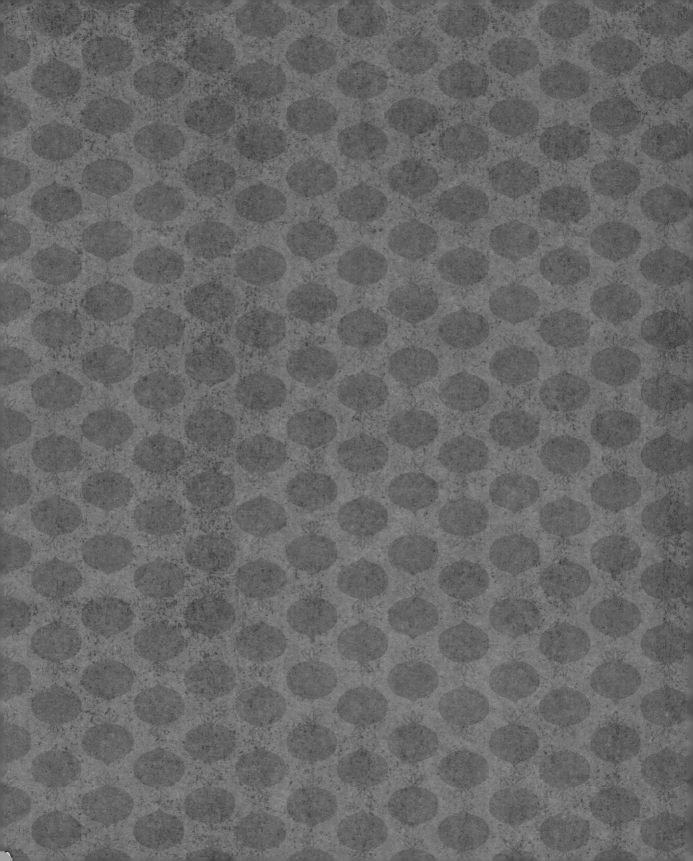

Resources

CLIMATE AND WEATHER

NOAA (National Oceanic and Atmospheric Administration)
ncdc.noaa.gov

USDA Hardiness Zone Map
planthardiness.ars.usda.gov

REGULATIONS FOR ORGANICALLY GROWN FOOD

OMRI (Organic Materials Review Institute)
omri.org

USDA, Alternative Farming Systems Information Center
nal.usda.gov/afsic/pubs/ofp/ofp.shtml

PESTS AND DISEASES

UC Davis Integrated Pest Management
ipm.ucdavis.edu/PMG/NE/index.html

BIOINTENSIVE GARDENING

Grow Biointensive
johnjeavons.info

SEED AND SUPPLIES

Baker Creek Heirloom Seeds
rareseeds.com

Bountiful Gardens
bountifulgardens.org

Cherry Gal Heirloom Seeds
cherrygal.com

Franchi Seeds of Italy
www.seedsofitaly.com

Heirloom Seeds
heirloomseeds.com

Irish Eyes Garden Seeds
irisheyesgardenseeds.com

Johnny's Selected Seeds
johnnyseeds.com

Native Seeds/SEARCH
nativeseeds.org

Peaceful Valley
groworganic.com

Seed Savers Exchange
seedsavers.org

Sustainable Seed Company
sustainableseedco.com

Territorial Seed Company
territorialseed.com

Veganic Agriculture Network
goveganic.net

Metric Conversions

INCHES	CENTIMETERS	INCHES	CENTIMETERS
¼	0.6	¼	0.6
½	1.3	½	1.3
¾	1.9	¾	1.9
1	2.5	1	2.5
2	5.1	2	5.1
4	10	4	10
6	15	6	15
8	20	8	20
10	25	10	25
12	30	12	30
18	46	18	46

TEMPERATURES

$$°C = 0.55 \times (°F - 32)$$
$$°F = (1.8 \times °C) + 32$$

Index

Main entries for Edibles A to Z appear in **bold** type.

About the Author

Geri Galian Miller, certified Master Gardener and horticulturist, is the founder of Home Grown Edible Landscapes, where her duties include consulting, designing, and overseeing the execution of edible and native landscaping for hospitality companies, restaurants, galleries, spas, and private residences. She has designed edible landscapes across Southern California for clients including mar'sel restaurant at Terranea Resort, Post & Beam, The Tasting Kitchen, Tender Greens, Scopa Italian Roots, Willie Jane, and Love & Salt. She is a member of the National Gardening Association, the California Native Plant Society, and the Theodore Payne Foundation. Miller is also a contributor to the *Huffington Post* and author of her own blog, *GroEdibles*. Visit her at groedibles.com.